Celebrating

ALL CREATURES
GREAT & SMALL

For the Love of the Yorkshire Dales

Celebrating
ALL CREATURES GREAT & SMALL
For the Love of the Yorkshire Dales

WRITTEN BY JAMES STEEN

FOREWORD BY ROSIE PAGE

Michael O'Mara Books Limited

First published in Great Britain in 2024 by
Michael O'Mara Books Limited
9 Lion Yard
Tremadoc Road
London SW4 7NQ

A CIP catalogue record for this book is available from the British Library.

ISBN: 978-1-78929-718-8 in hardback print format
ISBN: 978-1-78929-746-1 in ebook format

1 2 3 4 5 6 7 8 9 10

Cover design by Natasha Le Coultre
Printed and bound in Germany by Mohn Media Mohndruck

www.mombooks.com

CONTENTS

FOREWORD

My father's first sight of Swaledale, driving over Grinton Moor from Leyburn, was the start of a lifelong love affair with the Yorkshire Dales. He imparted this love of wild places to my brother, Jim, and me at a very early age, and enjoying the landscape and wildlife of North Yorkshire has played a huge part in both our lives. Dad, himself, found 'balm for the soul' on the high moorland.

Dad met and married my mother during wartime; my brother and I were born at a time when nobody had much money. As a family we had very little compared with the young in today's more materialistic world, but we were rich in the things that really mattered. We had our parents' unconditional love, attention and support, and lots of laughter. They taught us by example to work hard and play hard, and to enjoy the simple things which cost nothing, in particular an appreciation of the Yorkshire countryside and its wildlife. More than seventy years on, my pressed flowers still fall out of the pages of Dad's big veterinary textbooks – a poignant reminder of a wonderful childhood.

Fame never changed my dad. He regarded himself as 95 per cent vet, and 5 per cent author. He would mention that he was still top of the American bestseller list, then immediately change the subject to football. He was quiet, gentle, thoughtful and kind, always modest and a highly perceptive observer. He hated public speaking, but with his family and close friends he was a brilliant raconteur, and, of course, on paper he was hilarious.

Mum shunned the limelight even more, and Dad was very protective of her. She, too, had an excellent sense of humour. She was a born homemaker, a fantastic mother and a wonderfully supportive wife.

My parents seldom argued. The fact that as a six-year-old, I can remember their voices being raised while erecting a pulley over the Aga in our new home is testament to that. They were a true partnership – one was no good without the other. They had no need for big houses or big cars, and were content to spend most evenings in front of the TV with their dogs. One of their favourite programmes was *The Professionals* – they became friendly with the actor Lewis Collins, and even called their last dog, a border terrier, Bodie. They thoroughly enjoyed the original *All Creatures Great and Small*, of course, and both Chris Timothy and Robert Hardy became good friends.

This new series of *All Creatures* is, of course, an adaptation, and as such does not closely follow the stories in the Herriot books. But the ethos is right, the acting and production are superb, and we see it as sitting comfortably and respectfully alongside the books and the first series. Jim and I read the scripts, and at times give advice to help with the authenticity. The producers and cast are always extremely gracious to us and seem to welcome our input.

We were invited to watch the filming of 'our parents' getting married in a beautiful little church in Wharfedale – a surreal experience! I have had several Mums and Dads in film, theatre and TV. The early ones were, indeed, a few years older than me, while my new 'parents', Nick and Rachel, could be my grandchildren! Jim and I like them both very much. Nick has a head start with his Scottish accent, which is so similar to Dad's. Rachel actually looks just like old photos of Mum, and contacts me occasionally to ask me about her. Once she asked me if they would use endearments; they very much did not. Sometimes Mum would call the dog 'darling', and Dad would answer, 'Yes, dearest?', knowing fine well it was not him she was addressing.

One major difference is that Mum is portrayed as a hopeless cook. In fact, she was a terrific and innovative cook all her life, and when I was little, she would produce curries and spaghetti bolognese before most people had ever heard of them.

But speaking very generally, this new series is excellent, and it has encouraged a new generation to enjoy the works of James Herriot. It has also done an enormous amount to promote the Herriot name, which for many years has been a force for good. For decades it has helped tourism. Now it also helps small local charities of which he would hugely approve. Herriot Hospice Homecare is about to open a new hospice in Thirsk called Herriot Hospice at the Lambert, and the Yorkshire Dales Millennium Trust now has a James Herriot Plantation in Dad's favourite dale, Swaledale. He would be so proud.

This book is a great tribute to the new series, and to the Yorkshire Dales, its landscape and its people. The photos are marvellous, and the prose is informative and beautifully written. I see it as another contribution to Dad's greatest legacy – the joy and comfort that through his books and their adaptations he has given to tens of millions of people worldwide. It is my hope that this will continue in perpetuity.

Rosie Page
Daughter of James Herriot

INTRODUCTION

For so many of us, *All Creatures Great and Small* is simply compelling. Brilliantly written and with beautiful performances – by trained animals as well as by talented humans – the series, which is broadcast on Channel 5 in Britain and on PBS in the United States, is filmed in a luxuriously cinematic style. Wide, sweeping shots take us into the heart of the breathtaking Yorkshire countryside.

With its poignancy and humour, the show is pure escapism. It is the latest in a line of adaptations of James Herriot's memoirs by the BBC from the late 1970s to 1990, as well as two film dramatizations. Behind this series' success is a diverse team of crew and experts, from animal handlers, a consultant on-set vet and an animal welfare advisor to specialists in production design, costume design and prosthetics. Together – and with celebrated directors and producers – they create entertainment that takes us away from the harsh realities of our lives, the troubles of the world or just humdrum normality.

Frank Sinatra described the Hollywood musicals of the 1940s as 'fantasy trips' for cinema audiences. A moment to step away and to dream … Perhaps the same could be said of *All Creatures Great and Small*. Like a magic carpet, the show transports the viewer from anywhere in the world to the Yorkshire Dales of another era with its glorious, majestic scenery, as well as the glowing log-fire cosiness of Skeldale House and the buttery warmth of its kitchen. We watch *All Creatures* and feel good, even if we are also aware that much of it is set when the nation is at war.

This book is not merely a companion to the show but also an homage to Alf Wight, better known by his pen name, James Herriot. And, as the title suggests, this book is also a hearty toast to a spectacular part of northern England – the Yorkshire Dales.

With a landscape that can stop you dead in your tracks, not for nowt is Yorkshire known as 'God's own country'. The dales is a tapestry of endless rolling fields and hills, rivers and streams (or becks, as they often call them here), brooks and cascading waterfalls. It is a landscape of limestone gorges

and glens, heather-strewn moorland, and coves and caves that have been carved by time and hide secrets from the Ice Ages; of tarns and riggs and towering cliffs and enchanted moss-floored forests and fairytale woods – and all of them beneath a sky that can change in an instant from bright blue and radiant to black clouds and torrential downpour. It is not just any old sky but one that has been designated a Dark Sky Reserve, with large unpolluted areas; at nighttime it is coal-black except for its displays of meteors, the Milky Way and the Northern Lights.

From the high and windy points of the dales, the magnificent views are so powerful that for many centuries they have inspired artists, poets, writers, filmmakers and, of course, the producers of this adaptation, who regard the dales as a star of the show. Mind you, as the farmer Mr Dakin points out gruffly in the second episode of series four: 'Views don't pay bills … And you can't see much when it rains.' On that point, the weather is one of the many challenges for the production of *All Creatures*. The heavens can open at any moment and without warning signs.

There's that saying about never working with animals or children, although both are crucial to this show. The call sheet for day one of shooting was circulated among cast and crew, and it featured 'Misty the cat, Leo the cat, Jasper the cat, a rabbit, a tortoise and one small dog'. There was – as there always is – a tutor for the child actors, who might get to miss a day in class but still have to be diligent about their schoolwork.

The hero is James Herriot, who leaves his home in Glasgow to become a vet in Darrowby, a fictional small town in the dales. He lives in Skeldale House with Siegfried Farnon, a true English eccentric, and Siegfried's much younger brother Tristan (also known as Tris), an eternal optimist. Mrs Hall is the housekeeper but also the beating heart of the home. They are the 'family' at the centre of the story.

All Creatures is also a story of love and romance, primarily between James and farmer's daughter Helen Alderson. But there are the love stories of many others along the way. Above all else, it is a story about the love they have for each other, the world around them, as well for the wider community and the animals, with James and Helen's unshakeable love sitting reassuringly at the heart of the world.

Apart from family and friendship, love and romance, much of the humour comes from the chaos of the characters' adventures and their constant attempts to restore order. And there are other themes: home and away, and the hardship of the farming folk in the dales in Herriot's day. The central character, meanwhile, is the captivating landscape. This is North Yorkshire and the dales, where a spade's a spade, a brew is *the* cure-all, a minor victory in the day calls for a drop of Siegfried's 'good stuff' in the evening, and Sundays mean roast beef, Yorkshire puddings and a ladleful of piping-hot gravy. Alf Wight fell in love with the dales when he arrived and he remained in North Yorkshire for the rest of his life. His stories about the people, communities, ways of life, traditions, and the animals, all exist within this very particular and wonderful part of England. It is not just a setting; the stories are a part of the place itself.

'For if they fall, the one shall lift up the other.'

SIEGFRIED (FROM ECCLESIASTES 4:10)

ALF WIGHT

James Alfred Wight OBE, FRCVS – Alf to family, friends and clients – was the real James Herriot. He was born in Sunderland, Tyne and Wear, on 3 October 1916. His father, Jim, was a ship-plater, and his mother, Hannah, a dressmaker.

Alf spent the first twenty-three years of his life in Glasgow. After qualifying from Glasgow Veterinary College in 1939, he returned to the city of his birth, where he took his first post as a vet. He stayed there for six months before joining the practice at 23 Kirkgate in Thirsk in North Yorkshire, on the edge of the Yorkshire Dales. In 1941, Alf married Joan. They had two children, Jim (who, like his dad, qualified as a vet and worked at Skeldale House practice) and Rosie (who became a general practitioner).

Drawing on his experiences and the characters he had met, Alf started writing his first memoir in the mid-1960s, but then he rewrote, tinkered with and tweaked it, spending evenings tapping away on an Olivetti typewriter in front of the TV. In 1969, the manuscript for *If Only They Could Talk* was accepted and then published the following year. This was followed by *It Shouldn't Happen to a Vet*. These two memoirs were united in an omnibus edition for the US market under the title *All Creatures Great and Small* – the name stuck. He wrote eight Herriot memoirs, with total book sales estimated at 50 million.

As for his pen name, he required one because if he wrote under his real name, it would be seen as advertising and therefore a breach of the veterinary profession's rules and etiquette. He was watching a football match on television one evening when he was inspired by the Scottish goalkeeper who was playing for Birmingham City against Manchester United. He was a certain Jim Herriot. (Alf, by the way, was a lifelong supporter of Sunderland FC.)

James Herriot's books were first adapted for a BBC television series that began in the late 1970s. Despite his remarkable success as a writer, Alf remained a vet – the most

Top opposite: Alf Wight pictured with his beloved dog, Bodie.

Bottom opposite: Alf with his wife, Joan, working at home.

Below: Alf in his car with his dogs.

Top right: Alf at 23 Kirkgate, the real-life Skeldale House, where he lived and worked.

Bottom right: Alf signing copies of his bestselling book.

famous vet in the world – and lived in Yorkshire. Fans who made the Herriot pilgrimage and visited in the early days were often treated by Donald Sinclair to a guided tour of the veterinary practice.

Alf died aged seventy-eight on 23 February 1995. He was outlived by his beloved wife, Joan, his inspiration for the character of Helen Herriot. Alf's life is best captured and chronicled – and lovingly told – in his biography, *The Real James Herriot*. Published in 1999, it was written by his son Jim, today a retired vet.

THE YORKSHIRE DALES

James Herriot (and Alf) received letters of admiration from all over the world, and frequently they included the comment, 'I wish I could see the places you write about.'

The Yorkshire Dales are a series of 840 square miles of limestone hills and valleys, mostly in the county of North Yorkshire but also extending to the counties of Cumbria and Lancashire. They are set within the Pennines, a range of hills in northern England. *Dalr* was the Old Norse word for valley, and there are twenty main dales in Yorkshire. They include Wharfedale in the south (which is, incidentally, where *Calendar Girls* was filmed) and Dentdale in the north.

Further north, there is Swaledale and Wensleydale, where French monks settled a thousand years ago, bringing their cheese-making skills. BBC film crews came in the twentieth century, bringing their scripts for *All Creatures Great and Small*. The area is home to a diverse range of animals, birds and insects. Don't be alarmed if you see a brown bat with ears that are about three quarters the length of its body; that'll be – you've guessed it – the brown long-eared bat.

Some figures: the Yorkshire Dales National Park was established in 1954 and, as mentioned above, covers an area of 840 square miles. Within its boundaries there are about 1,600 miles of footpaths, as well as bridleways with a total distance of some 365 miles. The vets in the dales have their work cut out – there are 1,090 farms. Herriot writes of watching plough horses that were still used by farmers and yet to be replaced by tractors.

In the Middle Ages, merchants travelled from Italy to buy wool from places such as Bolton Priory and Fountains Abbey, while cattle have long provided milk, cheese and butter for England's north. The National Park provides important habitats for numerous species, and farmers help to manage this landscape, especially the hay meadows. While farming is a way of life for many in the dales, these uplands present a tough existence, both physically and economically. As so well portrayed in *All Creatures*, the daily challenges are gruelling.

'We were born to the land to work the land.'

JENNY ALDERSON

The National Park has its own Three Peaks (Whernside, Ingleborough and Pen-y-ghent), and every year thousands of walkers come to take up the challenge of completing the 24.5-mile circular route in twelve hours or less. Visitors who don't fancy the march have plenty more to do. They flock to Pendragon Castle in the Mallerstang Valley, or to Bolton Priory or Fountains Abbey, or to climb to the peaks of hills with quaint names, such as Lovely Seat.

You will never forget a drive along Buttertubs Pass, with its fantastic views of the surrounding valleys and fells as it crosses the moorland between Wensleydale and Swaledale from the small market town of Hawes to the hamlet of Thwaite. Why Buttertubs? Some say it's because the rocks here resemble butter tubs. Others recount a story about farmers who would stop for a breather on their way to market. To stop their butter melting on hot days, they lowered it into the cool, deep limestone potholes.

THE PLAYERS

The Ensemble Cast and Characters
of *All Creatures Great and Small*

NICHOLAS RALPH
PLAYS JAMES HERRIOT

Born in South Africa, Nick grew up in the seaside town of Nairn in the Scottish Highlands. The producers of *All Creatures* wanted a Scottish Herriot, as Alf Wight spoke with a Scottish burr. Nick received the call about auditioning for the role of James when he was performing at the National Theatre of Scotland – a mile from Glasgow Veterinary College, where Alf was a student. A good omen! Nick's mother and aunt were huge fans of Herriot, and his Uncle Henry had the entire collection of Herriot's books and, as a lad, went on a pilgrimage to the famous practice in Thirsk in order to meet Alf Wight.

SAMUEL WEST
PLAYS SIEGFRIED FARNON

Screen and stage actor, director and narrator, Samuel has starred in *Slow Horses*, *The Gentlemen*, *Darkest Hour* and *Mr Selfridge*. Siegfried Farnon is based on Donald Sinclair, who was first employer and then partner of Alf Wight at the veterinary practice at 23 Kirkgate, Thirsk. Donald was impatient, volatile, unpredictable and thoroughly decent. Samuel was drawn to the role partly because lead writer Ben Vanstone 'made the Siegfried character deeper, more complex, more flawed'.

ANNA MADELEY
PLAYS MRS HALL

Mrs Hall was a minor character in the Herriot books, her first name never mentioned. She was inspired by Mrs Weatherill, the housekeeper at Skeldale House. In the TV series Audrey Hall is a strong character who is the heart of the family, the moral core of the show. Enchantingly played by Anna, she keeps the men firmly grounded. Says Anna, 'Mrs Hall always means well and doesn't set out to stamp her values all over everybody else. She is a more nuanced, caring character, seeking out the goodness in others. She's no ordinary housekeeper.' During filming of the first series, Anna spent a lot of time with Ernie, the Golden Retriever who plays Jess, so they could bond.

CALLUM WOODHOUSE
PLAYS TRISTAN FARNON

Callum's first big role was as Leslie Durrell in the ITV adaptation of *The Durrells*. His character, Tristan, is based on Brian Sinclair, brother of Donald. Durham-born Callum says that Tristan has had a tough upbringing and 'tries to use humour as a barrier, and he's done it for so long that it sort of works for him. That's probably something that I do. Things may affect me, but more than I let on. I'm just a typical northern man: brush it off and get on with it.'

RACHEL SHENTON
PLAYS HELEN HERRIOT

'For me,' says Rachel, 'this show is as it is for the viewer – you just want to be there, be a part of it. It's like a warm blanket.' Helen was inspired by Gloucestershire-born Joan Danbury, who became Alf's wife, and they had two children, Jim and Rosie. Rachel's career has included creating and starring in *The Silent Child*, which she co-produced with her husband, Chris Overton. The short film was based on her own experiences as the child of a father who became deaf. At the 2018 Academy Awards it won an Oscar for Best Live Action Short Film.

JAMES ANTHONY-ROSE
PLAYS RICHARD CARMODY

Richard Carmody becomes the latest young vet to join Skeldale House and stands in for Tristan, who has left to fight for king and country. The character – novel to this adaptation – is a serious academic in his mid-twenties, always in a bow tie and usually with his nose deep in a textbook. While he is self-assured and high in IQ, his pedantic, awkward style, says James Anthony-Rose, is 'a kind of armour that he wears to protect himself from the things that he feels not so sure about, like his interpersonal skills'. An unimpressed Siegfried initially dismisses him: 'Richard Carmody, from London? He won't last.'

TONY PITTS
PLAYS RICHARD ALDERSON

As father to Helen and Jenny, Richard is a hardworking farmer and a widower who often seems preoccupied, perhaps deep in thought as he reflects on the loss of his wife. Tony, who was born and raised in Sheffield, is a working-class northern lad. He made his name in *Emmerdale*, playing the loveable rogue Archie Brooks. In *Peaky Blinders* he was Sergeant Moss, and in *Line of Duty* he played Detective Chief Superintendent Les Hargreaves.

MATTHEW LEWIS
PLAYS HUGH HULTON

Dashing and debonair, Matthew has also played a diverse range of roles. He was the wand-wielding Neville Longbottom in the *Harry Potter* films, and in *All Creatures* he is wealthy landowner Hugh Hulton and Helen's fiancé (though not for as long as he may have hoped). Hugh is posh but, as Matthew says, 'also warm-hearted, approachable, not stand-offish. Although he was born and bred in Yorkshire, he went to a boarding school in London and doesn't have a Yorkshire accent.' To help master the accent, Matthew, who was born in Leeds, says, 'I watched a lot of *Blackadder*, particularly *Blackadder Goes Forth*.'

IMOGEN CLAWSON
PLAYS JENNY ALDERSON

'Jenny is a strong, independent female and I am honoured to play her,' says Imogen, who had just turned twelve years old when she joined the cast of *All Creatures*. She lives in Harrogate and was unaware of Herriot – her parents were devotees, however, and excitedly filled her in before the audition. Imogen's role, in fact, was new, as Jenny did not feature in Herriot's books. This young actress's favourite musical is *Hamilton*, and she has been inspired by Emma Watson and Sadie Sink. But can either of them boast that they've clipped a sheep's toenails?

PATRICIA HODGE OBE
PLAYS MRS PUMPHREY

Patricia took over the role from Dame Diana Rigg, who very sadly died in September 2020. Mrs Pumphrey is a typically English eccentric and kind-hearted widow who lives with her pampered Pekingese, Tricki Woo – and a regiment of servants – in the grandeur of Pumphrey Manor (the location is Broughton Hall). The character was mostly inspired by Miss Warner, who lived in the village of Sowerby, a couple of miles from the Sinclair-Wight practice in Thirsk. Patricia says, 'Mrs Pumphrey is one of those people we all know – dotty in a delightful way.' Mrs Pumphrey sees the world in terms of Tricki. 'She is also a woman of considerable means and wherewithal. The only thing she needs is somebody to help her with Tricki and make sure he is all right.'

'All the world's a stage, and all the men and women merely players.

They have their exits and their entrances; And one man in his time plays many parts ...'

AS YOU LIKE IT, WILLIAM SHAKESPEARE

HOME AND AWAY

Arailway guard blows his whistle and the steam train blows its horn as it chug-chugs out of the station, its wheels slowly gathering momentum. This is Glasgow, and it's 1937. James Herriot senior and his wife, Hannah – with young James's dog, Don – watch from the platform as the train pulls away. 'Oh, I hope to God he gets it,' says Hannah of her son's interview for a job at the veterinary practice in the Yorkshire Dales town of Darrowby. For the journey, she's packed James off with a small brown bag filled with sandwiches, and as for her final words to him before they hug farewell and he boards – 'Cheese and pickle. Here's your ticket. Now get on before you miss it.'

The journey from Glasgow's Queen Street station to Thirsk – the market town that partly inspired Darrowby – takes about four and a half hours. First you travel east to Edinburgh, then change and take another train south, down along the north-east coastline of England. Look out on one side and there's the North Sea, and you can see Holy Island (also known as Lindisfarne), believed to be the first place in England where Vikings landed in the ninth century. The train skirts the Northumberland coastline, passing ancient towns that include Bamburgh and Alnwick with their eleventh-century castles.

There's certainly plenty to see, and it's a lengthy but memorable adventure, from the imposing rural landscape to the cityscape of Newcastle – not far from Sunderland, birthplace of Alf Wight – and then passing Durham and Darlington and disembarking at Northallerton. The final part of the journey requires taking either a train or – like hopeful James – a bus from Northallerton to Thirsk. Either way, it's a long old journey from Glasgow, and by the time the young vet reached his destination there would have been nothing but a few breadcrumbs in the bottom of that brown bag from Mum.

'Home is where the heart is. Is it not, James?' That's the question Hannah asks of her son later on, in the first episode of series two. By then James's heart is firmly in Darrowby and the Yorkshire Dales, a couple of hundred miles from Glasgow.

'Home is where the heart is. Is it not, James?'

HANNAH HERRIOT

And by then he has met and fallen in love with Helen. The longer he worked in Darrowby, wrote Herriot, the more 'beguiled' he became by 'the charms of the Yorkshire Dales'. But the Second World War would temporarily deprive him of these charms, as he signed up for the Royal Air Force.

Alf Wight did not entirely base Darrowby on Thirsk; he saw his fictional town as a composite of towns in and around the Yorkshire Dales, including Richmond and Leyburn. Thirsk is attractive and full of character, described by Alf (writing as James Herriot in *James Herriot's Yorkshire*) as 'a happy town. It has a cheerful aspect with its cobbled square and its fretted line of roofs set off by the long ridge of the Hambleton Hills.' A corner of this happy town was transformed for the series, taking it back to the thirties, creating a clothes shop and a motor sales shop, and archive references were used to make the Ritz cinema look as it did in 1938, recreating the original sign and ticket office. The show's production designer Jackie Smith says, 'The locals seemed delighted.'

The Sutton Bank escarpment is 5 miles due east of Thirsk. Looking out over the Vale of York and the Vale of Mowbray, you can see what Alf meant when he described Sutton Bank as the 'finest view in England'. He remains here today: following his funeral, his family gathered at this spot and scattered his ashes.

Perhaps it is fitting that Sutton Bank, the highest point of the Hambleton Hills, has been the setting for so many stories over the centuries. A fort stood there during the Iron Age, and in 1322 this was the site of the Battle of Byland. King Edward II's army was defeated by Scottish king Robert the Bruce, whose troops forced their way up to win what was literally an uphill battle. In the mid-1930s the hill was home to a glider club and German pilots were trained there.

Sutton Bank became a site of excavation in 2024, as archeologists began a three-year investigation to help learn key information about this place that was so special to Alf. And special to his dogs, because frequently they came to be walked here in between their master's daily house and farm visits. 'I must have stopped at this spot thousands of times because there is no better place for a short stroll,' wrote Herriot in his 1993 book about Yorkshire and its landscape. 'Along the green path which winds round the hill's edge, with the fresh wind swirling and that incredible panorama beneath.'

He regarded Swaledale as the most beautiful part of England, and he saw Richmond – at the foot of that dale, with its Norman castle, fourteenth-century church and cobbled alleys – as 'just about the most romantic and charming town in the country'. Alf was fascinated by the history of the ancient church of St Mary's.

Within the graveyard there is a stone that commemorates the deaths of more than a thousand people who lost their lives to the plagues of the sixteenth and seventeenth centuries. And then there is the story of Robert Willance. He was hunting on Whitcliffe Scar one day in 1606 when a mist descended and his horse bolted and ran off the edge of the scar … Together, man and beast fell 200 feet. The horse died in the fall, and

'It feels strange hearing you call somewhere else home. You belong here. This is your home.'

HELEN TO JAMES

Overleaf: Alf Wight in the Yorkshire Dales.

Willance suffered a serious leg injury and later had to have the limb amputated. He had the leg buried in the cemetery. Willance was reunited with it a decade later.

Thirsk does not have the village feel of Darrowby, which, of course, is fictional. Head to Grassington and that's far more like Herriot's Darrowby (which is ideal, as that is the location for the series). Thirsk, however, certainly has the spirit of Herriot. You cannot help but think of Alf Wight and James Herriot as you stroll from Market Place along Kirkgate and then reach number 23. How many times did Alf Wight walk this same route as he made his way to the surgery after house and farm calls? For many years number 23 was the veterinary practice at which Alf worked – and the home he shared – with Donald Sinclair. Donald's younger brother, Brian – the inspiration for Tristan – had yet to qualify, and also lived there.

The building was also the inspiration for Skeldale House, the fictional practice and the place where Siegfried, Tristan, Mrs Hall and James (and later Helen) live together. Herriot wrote of the practice, with ivy 'hanging in untidy profusion across its old bricks'. Today it is a museum, the World of James Herriot (also known as the Herriot Centre), dedicated to the author, his books, the two films, the original BBC series and this most recent adaptation.

Every week and from every corner of the world, Herriot fans come on a pilgrimage to visit this particular World. Step through the door of the museum and it is like stepping back in time. The ground floor of

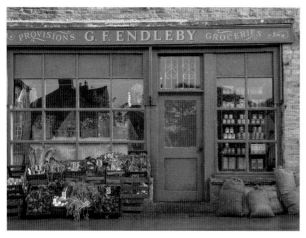

the museum has been lovingly and skilfully restored to its former self, a replica of what was once the Sinclair-Wight veterinary practice, complete with the labyrinthine layout of its winding passage that leads from the front door through the hallway and down to the kitchen and then the scullery. It's impressive, and it helped to inspire the set of Skeldale, which was designed by Jackie Smith and built inside an old disused mill. Jackie has borrowed items from the museum to use as props for her set.

Visitors to the museum and to the set can almost smell Mrs Hall's freshly baked scones or the waft of the crackling logs on the fire in the sitting room and perhaps get a whiff of smoke from Siegfried's pipe and hear his voice bellowing 'Door!' or 'Phone's ringing!' The set and the World of James Herriot feature a Bakelite telephone – the sort that was common in the 1930s – and on it is written the number:

Alf Wight, left, and Nick Ralph, our hero Herriot.

Darrowby 2297. This was the telephone number for the real Sinclair-Wight practice.

Rachel Shenton talks of going above and beyond to get the fabric and the DNA right and of how she loves the way the set – carefully plotted and planned, and adorned with artifacts from the World of James Herriot – has a feeling of familiarity. 'When I first emerged in my costume it was like being transported back in time. With the late thirties all around me, I couldn't help but feel I'd stepped into that era.'

As Alf Wight discovered when he first arrived in 1940, Thirsk is a small town, divided in two by the River Codbeck. The town's name is believed to originate from the old British words *tre*, meaning town, and *isk*, meaning river or brook.

Thirsk is in the Vale of Mowbray, named after the de Mowbray family, which was granted the land in the late eleventh century by William the Conqueror. A community was established around de Mowbray's Thirsk Castle, which may have preceded the Norman Conquest by about a century and was described as 'a noble pile of a building, uniting the magnificence of a royal palace with the strength and security of a baronial fortress'.

However, it was within these castle walls in the twelfth century that Sir Roger de Mowbray conspired with William, King of the Scots, to mount a rebellion against Henry II. The revolt was soon suppressed, but de Mowbray's castle was snatched from him and, under Henry's orders, destroyed. If an Englishman's home is his castle, Roger now had neither. He was spared his life and did not lose his freedom. Instead, he went on a crusade to the Holy Land, where he died.

On the east side is what was once known as Old Thirsk, and it has a square, St James Green. For many years this square was dominated by a wondrous wych elm tree, so large that even the voting for the town's member of parliament took place beneath its weeping branches. It's said that Henry Percy, the fourth earl of Northumberland, died beneath this tree when, in 1489, he was attacked by rioters protesting against his hike in taxes as part of what is known as the Yorkshire rebellion. Most of Britain's elm were wiped out by Dutch elm disease, a fungal infection spread by bark beetles, which arrived in this country in the 1960s.

The demise of the ancient elm in Thirsk, however, was not due to disease but to a group of mischievous lads. They set light to the tree on Bonfire Night, 5 November 1818. After that blaze, what remained of the tree was just enough to make two chairs for the lord of the manor, John Bell.

Zooming forward 123 years to the day, Alf and Joan were married in St Mary's Church – on Kirkgate, a stone's throw from the veterinary practice and a five-minute walk from St James Green and on the other side of the Codbeck – on 5 November 1941, the year before Alf joined the Royal Air Force. (Subsequently, Joan gave birth to the couple's children, first Jim and then Rosie, in a nursing home on St James Green.) Mr and Mrs Wight spent their honeymoon at the Wheatsheaf in Carperby in the Yorkshire Dales, an inn that dates back to the early 1800s and is about a mile from the waterfalls at Aysgarth. Actually, they didn't spend it there entirely, as Alf combined the early days of his marriage with tuberculosis testing on farms in the dales. The dairy industry

'Dear Mum and Dad, I'm enjoying my stay in Darrowby. It's very different from home.'

EVA, THE EVACUEE, WRITES TO HER PARENTS

was severely hit by tuberculosis, and it was not just cows which suffered. TB could be passed to humans through infected milk. Donald Sinclair, who had married young when he was at veterinary college, lost his wife to the disease.

One day Melissa Gallant, the executive producer, phoned Jim and Rosie to ask, 'Would you like to come and watch your mother and father getting married?' The nuptials were being reenacted for the screen, with Nick Ralph and Rachel Shenton playing the happy couple, James and Helen (based on Alf and Joan). Back in 1941, with the nation at war and travel being difficult, there was only a handful of guests to witness the marriage. Donald Sinclair was the best man, and Joan was given away by a friend who worked with her at the mill. Only the four of them and the vicar were present.

Above: Alf Wight and his wife, Joan.

Below: Watching their parents get married. Alf Wight's children, Jim Wight and Rosie Page, on set on the wedding day.

The on-screen wedding day for James and Helen is attended by just a small number, though the bride arrives with her dad in Mrs Pumphrey's Rolls-Royce. In the front seat, Mrs Hall has Tricki on her lap and doesn't seem to be completely thrilled by this turn of events. Siegfried hops into the church with one shoe on and the other one in his hand, and Clancy, the dog, has swallowed the ring. At the altar, Siegfried presents James and Helen with a ring made from knotted string, which was courtesy of Mrs Hall's quick thinking.

The Wights' honeymoon hotel, the Wheatsheaf, brims with pride at its connection to Alf, and it's difficult to enter without noticing the plaque on the outside wall: 'The Wheatsheaf. James Herriot's honeymoon stay. (1941).' It is also said that six weeks later, the Hollywood star Greta Garbo stayed at the same inn after an evening of singing to the troops at Catterick Garrison.

Market towns were established many centuries ago. In medieval times the king granted a charter to hold a market, and the marketplace was indicated by a large cross, obelisk or spire. Thirsk market square in medieval times contained a market cross, which was 9 feet high and stood atop four stone steps. At some point a sundial was added. Over the centuries, however, it was knocked and battered and eroded so that eventually it was not much more than a stump on steps. In 1893, the people of Thirsk wondered how best to commemorate the impending marriage of Queen Victoria's grandson, the Duke of York, to Queen Mary of Teck. The residents decided to erect a clock in the place of the market cross, so the old, eroded monument was moved to another part of the square. In his books, Herriot writes of a clock in Darrowby's Market Place; another nod to Thirsk.

If you want to see a good example of a market cross, head to Ripley, which is just north of Harrogate and on the edge of Nidderdale, a thirty-minute drive from Thirsk. In Market Place in Ripley, the market cross stands on four steps that are a few metres wide and is right beside a jolly inn, the Boar's Head, and a few minutes' walk from Ripley Castle. You might

'Life never goes the way you think it does. If it did, I wouldn't be here on my own expecting a child while my husband goes off to war. Come to think of it, I'd probably be married to Hugh Hulton.'

HELEN TO MRS HALL

do a double-take when you see the castle – it's the location for the restaurant, the Renniston, which features in a couple of series. Siegfried whisks Diana Brompton to the Renniston, and when James is wondering where to take Helen on a date, Tristan advises, 'You should take her to the Renniston. Trust me, women like to be wined and dined. And nothing says *be mine* quite like a lobster thermidor.'

When Thirsk's market cross was moved, a 30-feet-high clock was erected in its place, complete with a spire and a drinking fountain beside it – although the timing of the clock was not perfect. It wasn't erected until 1896, by which stage George and Mary were celebrating their third wedding anniversary, and he was that bit closer to becoming

King George V. Ever since those days this market cross has been a local landmark, though over the years it has been renovated and restored. Around the point when Alf arrived in Thirsk in 1940, the clock's mechanism was altered so it could operate electronically, and the water fountain was removed.

For centuries, every Monday has been a market day in Thirsk, and the tradition continues, though if you had visited before the mid-1800s, you'd have seen 'the shambles'. This was the slaughterhouse, and every market square had its shambles. You can just picture it in Darrowby. The shambles was a public place where cattle, sheep and poultry were slaughtered and butchered in preparation for sale.

'You're a lucky girl, you know. You won't find better.'
HANNAH HERRIOT

'I'm sure he won't, neither.' HELEN

WESLEY AND YORKSHIRE

Alf's parents, James and Hannah, were married in 1915 at the Primitive Methodist Church in Sunderland, where his father was an organist. Alf was raised in a Methodist household – no drinking, no gambling, no swearing – and in Herriot's books there is at least one reference to 'an upright Methodist'. Methodism was introduced to Thirsk – and much of England – by the Rev. John Wesley, who spent decades of the eighteenth century touring the country, preaching the gospel and gathering supporters for his cause. Often, he and his followers were set upon by angry mobs. Wesley kept a diary of his travels and adventures (*The Journal of the Reverend John Wesley*), and in volume two, his entry for Tuesday 21 April 1747 reads: 'I called at Thirsk; but, finding the town full of holiday folks, drinking, cursing, swearing, and cockfighting, did not stop at all, but rode on to Boroughbridge, and in the afternoon to Leeds.'

Not so much Thirsk as Thirst. It had a pub on every corner of Market Place – the Black Bull, the White Swan, the Red Bear, the Blacksmith's Arms, the Crown Inn, the King's Arms, the Three Tuns. (Drunkenness was not always tolerated and, like the minor theft of, say, a coat or trousers, could be punishable with a lengthy spell in jail.)

Wesley's persistence paid off: his preaching skills were rewarded, and in 1816 the Methodists built a new place of worship on St James Green. (The Quakers, meanwhile, had a meeting place and a burial ground in Kirkgate.) Wesley was not an unfamiliar face in this part of Yorkshire. In a journal entry for 1759, he records: 'At seven in the evening I preached to an immense congregation at the foot of a high mountain near Otley.' He was frequently met with violence and hostility, and it's a wonder that the Methodist leader lived to the age of eighty-seven, when he died peacefully.

'I love it here. Every day is different, I wake up and have no idea where the job will take me. I might be up in the High Dales wrestling cattle, or rescuing a dog that's had its paw caught in a trap … It's my home.'

JAMES

MUSICAL INTERLUDE

John Wesley's younger brother, Charles, was a prolific writer of hymns. Prolific is wildly understating his accomplishments. He wrote some 6,500 songs to be sung in church. It was Cecil Frances Alexander (1818–1895) whose work inspired the American publishers to come up with titles for Herriot's books, later to be used for the screen adaptations. Known as Fanny to her friends and family, the Dublin-born hymn writer, poet and devout Christian composed the lyrics of 'There Is a Green Hill Far Away' and the Christmas carol 'Once in Royal David's City'. In 1848, Fanny saw the publication of her book *Hymns for Little Children*. It contained the following hymn, which in 1887 was set to music composed by William Henry Monk, who, like Alf's father, was an English organist. The hymn is now known around the world, and the four lines of the first verse provided the titles of four omnibus editions of Herriot's books.

> All things bright and beautiful,
> All creatures great and small,
> All things wise and wonderful,
> The Lord God made them all.

The year of John Wesley's death, 1791, was also the year of the birth of the veterinary profession in Britain. You can almost hear Donald Sinclair talking about the origins of his profession and how we cannot think of it without reference to a horse called Eclipse. He was an exemplary thoroughbred, who in the flat-racing seasons of 1769 and 1770 was unbeaten on courses such as Epsom and Newmarket. Eclipse had amazing speed and stride, as well as limitless endurance over long distances. He was put to stud and died in 1789, aged twenty-five, an undisputed champion, and he would become the ancestor of many more champions.

Undefeated thoroughbred racehorse Eclipse, *c.*1770.

What had caused the death of this famous horse, and why was he so phenomenally successful during his racing career? Partly to help answer these questions, a committee was formed with the intention of establishing a veterinary school. As a nation, we needed to learn more about animal disease, and leading the way was a Frenchman who was the only qualified vet in the country, Charles Benoit Vial de St Bel. The Odiham Agricultural Society also supported the campaign.

And so in 1791, the Veterinary College, London, was built in the parish of St Pancras, occupying what is today the site of the Royal Veterinary College. It all began with four students, who embarked on a three-year course that covered all elements

'The Royal Veterinary College, 1825'.

of veterinary work. From its roots as a horse infirmary the college flourished and grew to become a science-based institution. In 1875, Queen Victoria granted the college its first Charter of Incorporation.

As for Eclipse and his legacy, it is said that more than nine out of ten thoroughbreds in the twenty-first century can trace their descent to him in the male line. Writing in the *Guardian* in 2007, the author and journalist Nicholas Clee noted that in the previous year's Epsom Derby, every horse was a male line descendant of Eclipse, as was every horse that ran in the French Derby and the Kentucky Derby.

Baines' History and Directory of the 1820s noted that the countryside surrounding Thirsk 'is rich and delightful and all tourists concur in the opinion that the vale of Mowbray, of which Thirsk is pretty nearly the centre, is scarcely to be equalled by any tract of country in the kingdom, for fertility, expansion and picturesque scenery'. Had you come to Thirsk at around this time you would have found (apart from the busy pubs) a small town with plenty of dales folk coming for one thing or another.

Baines' directory paints a picture of the town as it once was. It's a bit like a precursor to the *Yellow Pages*, showing that a whole host of tradespeople and services could be found in Thirsk – academies, attorneys, bakers, blacksmiths, buckle makers, butchers, boot and shoemakers, cabinet-makers, cattle dealers, confectioners, ironmongers and various makers of gloves, guns, baskets, breeches, chairs, chains, dresses, hats, perfume, rope and twine, watches and clocks. There were merchants of brandy and porter. There were tallow chandlers (who made candles) and maltsters (who produced malt for brewing beer). There were brewers too, making something just as potent as the lethal beer made by farmer Bert Sharpe in *All Creatures*. As Tristan says to Mrs Hall: 'You can lead a horse to water, Mrs H. But you can't make it guzzle six pints of Sharpe's brew.'

Thirsk was home to some fourteen tailors, three of them in Kirkgate, where shops included a few grocers. On the same street a certain Jane Rowntree dealt in glass, china and earthenware, while Elizabeth Armstrong sold confectionery. Pubs included the King's Arms and the Mason's Arms, along with a couple of butcher shops and two breweries. Of the six farmers living in town, five of them lived in St James Green. Kirkgate also had a few tea dealers. And remember, this tea was not in bags. Samuel West recalls receiving a letter after the first series of *All Creatures*. 'Somebody wrote to me, saying, "You were all having tea without a tea strainer." I realized – oh yes, in 1937 we were about fifteen years away from having tea bags. I wrote back, "I promise you there will be a tea strainer in series two." For me, that's the big difference between the first and second series. The tea strainer in the second but not the first.'

There were four surgeons in Thirsk in the 1820s. However, there was at that time only one veterinary surgeon. Just one, and he seems to have been a part-time vet. His name was Thomas Johnson, 'dealer in oils and paint, and veterinary surgeon', and he was on the north side of Market Place.

But let's return to our veterinary surgeons and their companions in Darrowby. The logs are ablaze in the sitting-room fireplace. It is Christmas time at Skeldale House – the Christmas episode of series two. The residents of the house are gathered beside the fire. James – with Helen and Tristan next to him, and Siegfried and Mrs Hall in comfy chairs – is kneeling in front of the fire and holding a log that he has carved. It's called a *Cailleach*, a traditional Yule log in which the face of Old Woman Winter is whittled into the wood. 'It's a family tradition,' says James. 'Every year we burn a Christmas log to bring prosperity and good luck for the year to come.'

'I think we could all do with a bit of that,' says Mrs Hall, and James lays the log on the fire.

'Ungracious, parsimonious, pea-brained neanderthals, that whole bloody family! They call me out on a Saturday night, belittle my professional opinion and then have the audacity to claim I've interrupted their family dinner.'

SIEGFRIED, RETURNING FROM A HOUSE CALL

'What happens now?' asks Siegfried. 'Some kind of pagan chant or something?'

'Close,' replies James before explaining the ritual. 'My dad always quotes a verse of Rabbie Burns. I hope you don't mind …' And as the log catches, he recites Robert Burns's familiar verses. 'Should auld acquaintance be forgot, and never brought to mind? Should auld acquaintance be forgot, and days of auld lang syne?' We see the faces of the characters as they listen to James reciting the words.

'For auld lang syne, my dear, for auld lang syne. We'll take a cup o' kindness yet, for days of auld lang syne …' The poem, sung as an anthem of the New Year, is poignant, epitomizing family, togetherness and friendship. It is an evocative scene as well because we know – and the characters do not – that war is looming. The ringing of wedding bells for James and Helen is coming soon, but so too is the wail of air-raid sirens.

Or maybe it will be a marriage without the ringing of wedding bells. Towards the end of episode six in the third series, Siegfried and Mrs Hall are standing by the market square, with the Skeldale dogs, Jess and Dash, at their feet. James and Tristan have gone to the army recruitment office. 'Do you think the bells will stop ringing, like in the Great War? Do you remember?' says Mrs Hall. Siegfried, reflective, nods. 'Every bell in the country,' he says. 'From Land's End to John O'Groats. Completely silent till the armistice.'

'I wonder when we shall hear them again,' she says, and Siegfried takes her hand in his. As the script says, 'No words necessary. He's there for her.' At the window of Skeldale House we see Helen, looking down at James in the square below. Her eyes are filled with both sadness and pride.

Sometimes the world beyond Darrowby and the dales holds a dark secret that belongs to one of the characters, and it's a secret that has been buried for years. There is, for instance, that moment in episode two of the first series when we see Mrs Hall, sitting at the table in her scullery, writing a cheque for two pounds and carefully printing the name: Edward Hall. She folds the cheque inside a written letter and puts it into a package along with a paper bag of sweets and some biscuits that she's baked.

Bit by bit, little by little, we will learn about her son, Edward, and their relationship. As the story develops in the series, we see that she writes to him, makes gifts for him, sets money aside for him. All of these are sent to Edward … only to be later returned by the postman to Mrs Hall at Skeldale House. We learn that Edward stole from his mother's previous employer in another part of Yorkshire. Mrs Hall reported the crime to the police and left that employer. And that is the what, where, when, why and how she ended up in Darrowby and at Skeldale House. Edward, like his father, Robert, is an absent character: we know he exists, but for now we do not see him. 'Not known at this address'

is scrawled across the post when it is returned to Mrs Hall. She wants to patch things up, yet it seems he does not want to see her … Until they meet at the railway station – their brief encounter.

Eva Feldman (played by Ella Bernstein) is the young evacuee who leaves her home in Manchester and comes to stay with the family at Skeldale House (in the Christmas episode of the third series). Siegfried reassures Eva: 'It's all right to miss home. You're allowed to cry.'

'Away' is the train departing, either from Darrowby, which is shot at Oakworth station, or Glasgow railway station (Keighley). 'Away' is on the other side of the English Channel, and the Great War in which Siegfried and Dalesmen fought, and throughout the series there are references to the conflict. These build up to the dramatic opening to the third episode of series three: a flashback to Siegfried's experiences of the horrors of the Great War. A young Siegfried (Andy Sellers) is an officer on the mustard-gassed battlefields of Ypres. An army horse is saved, but later Siegfried is ordered by Major Sebright Saunders (Jolyon Coy) to shoot it and the other horses. That way they won't need to be transported across the Channel as the war ends. They'll be sold for horse meat, says the commanding officer.

The war ended in 1918, some twenty years before James arrives in Darrowby, but its effects continued to resonate. There were men who had not returned, and the ones who made it back often had severe disabilities after having limbs amputated or suffering shellshock.

There was mistrust of authority. In a scene with James, Helen's dad, Richard Alderson (played by Tony Pitts), remembers the impact of the Great War: 'The government let anyone go and fight. Farmers, miners, doctors, vets. And do you know what happened? The whole bloody country ground to a halt. And then halfway through the war things started to come undone and I were working all hours. I couldn't get the help. And there weren't a day went by that I weren't scared out of my wits we'd have enough food to feed our Helen.

Took bloody ages to recover just because some pompous pen-pusher thought they knew best.' (As an aside, for series two, Jackie Smith and her team built a set for Heston Grange, home of the Aldersons. 'In the story Mrs Alderson passed away some years previously,' says Jackie, 'and since then all attention has been on the working of the farm. It leaves little time for niceties and thought for decoration.' The kitchen has paint-washed plaster walls and old Georgian cupboards with a blackened range and flagstone floors, and the colour palette features the colours of the earth.)

Travel through the dales today and you will see memorials and tributes to those who fell on the battlefield. Aysgarth – set within farmland and forests in Upper Wensleydale – is well-known for its many waterfalls, especially the dramatic Aysgarth Falls, which cascade over three steps in the River Ure. But go into the village and there's a memorial with a plaque that bears the names of the three villagers who lost their lives in the Great War: James P. Bell, William Hemsley and John Percival. Villagers gathered together to carry stone from a nearby quarry to build it. Three is a low number, but it also might have represented about 10 per cent of a small village's male population.

Thornton Rush is a couple of miles from Aysgarth, and there the Thornton Rush Institute was built in 1924 to commemorate four village men who served for their country … and never returned.

Or take a trip to Gunnerside, where, in the grounds of the Methodist church, a stone memorial commemorates seven local men who died in the First World War (and two who lost their lives in the Second World War). Meanwhile the beautiful village of Langcliffe sits beside the River Ribble, just north of Settle and east of Giggleswick. There, you'll see the old water fountain that served the village for a couple of centuries. Shortly after the Great War, this local landmark was adapted to become a memorial, and it bears a cross made of stone along with the names of eleven village men killed during the First World War (later to be joined by the names of the four village men killed during the Second World War).

'It's times like this which remind me how grateful I am for everything I have … Not the practice, or the house or the beautiful countryside, or any other thing. It's the people. Infuriating as you all are, I'm rather fond of you. And, well, there's that – so, well … Merry bloody Christmas.'

SIEGFRIED

A railway guard and the steam train blew their whistles, and the train chugged out of Leeds railway station, heading north towards the dales. On board were the Leeds Pals. Their story is heartbreaking but a key piece of the history of the dales in the Great War.

At the outbreak of war, in the summer of 1914, a British army was needed, and it would be known as Kitchener's New Army. These units were raised by local authorities and private institutions that supplied clothing, billeting and food, while the army provided weapons and training. Volunteers were spurred on by patriotism and by posters that were plastered throughout the country and featured Lord Kitchener, the moustachioed and macho Secretary of State for War, alongside rallying words. The most iconic poster showed Kitchener pointing his finger at the viewer, with the message: 'Britons Lord Kitchener wants you'. Think of the opening scenes of episode one of the third series: at a notice board we see a soldier pinning up an army recruitment poster that shows a young man in army uniform holding a football under his arm, with the words: 'THE FINEST JOB IN THE WORLD. WORK AND PLAY ALL OVER THE GLOBE. JOIN THE ARMY.'

Young men signed up together in groups of friends so they could serve together, side by side. Each of these military divisions had its own regimental name, but they became known as the 'pals' of different regions of the country. Lord Derby created the phrase after organizing a successful recruitment campaign in Liverpool. He addressed the new recruits and said they should be known as a 'battalion of pals'.

The soldiers in the newly formed 15th Battalion (1st Leeds) West Yorkshire Regiment were known as the Leeds Pals, and the battalion was made up of about 1,300 troops. One morning the Pals boarded the train at Leeds and travelled about 50 miles north, beyond Harrogate and into the dales countryside. They disembarked at Masham railway station and then marched 5 miles to a training camp at Breary Banks, near the hamlet of Colsterdale. There was

The iconic First World War recruitment poster.

already an established camp here, on the eastern edge of the dales, because about a decade earlier hundreds of navigators had been brought to this same spot to build reservoirs. The workers lived in huts, which were still intact and habitable for the Leeds Pals. There was a supply of fresh water from the reservoirs, and food and materials could be brought via the railway.

In the summer of 1915 the battalion became part of 93 Brigade in the 31st Division of the Fourth Army – every battalion was formed of Pals. They were sent first to Egypt to defend the Suez Canal as part of the Imperial Strategic Reserve. In March 1916, they sailed to France to play a part in the Battle of the Somme. In the assault on the German lines on 1 July 1916, following an intense artillery bombardment, 31st Division was to attack and take the village of Serre. At 7.30 a.m. on 1 July, the Pals moved out of the trenches and advanced. They were decimated by German machine-gun fire and artillery. Within minutes of battle every officer was killed or wounded, 233 other ranks were killed or later died of wounds and 267 were left wounded. Some 181 troops were missing. Only 47 soldiers were uninjured. On the first day, 209 Leeds Pals were killed; among the dead was Horace Iles, who had enlisted at the age of fourteen, lying about his age to fight for king and country.

Set back from the road and looking out onto the fields of Breary Banks there is a stone memorial. It marks the lives, bravery and, ultimately, the sacrifice of the Leeds Pals. After the war, one of the surviving soldiers, Private A. V. Pearson, said that 'the date of 1st July is engraved deep in our hearts, along with the faces of our Pals, a grand crowd of chaps. We were two years in the making and ten minutes in the destroying …'

Those who fell at the Battle of the Somme included young Sergeant Wight, of the 19th Battalion of the Durham Light Infantry. When a boy was born three months later, his parents named him Alfred – Alf – after this man, his uncle, who had sacrificed his life.

'Mam used to say everyone's fighting a battle you know nothing about. Which is why you must always be kind.'

HELEN

A bus rolls into town, and two passengers clamber off. It is James Herriot – but James senior this time – and he is with his wife, Hannah. Young James is there to meet his parents, who have made that journey from their home in Glasgow via train and then the bus – perhaps the same one on which James first met Helen. Mr and Mrs Herriot are here for the wedding – to witness the marriage of the next Mr and Mrs Herriot. 'You're too young to be getting married,' says Hannah to James as she gives him a hug. 'You should still be at home with your mammy.' And James's dad says, 'He'd be an old man before he got wed if it was up to you.'

FAMILY AND FRIENDSHIP

Family forms the foundations of *All Creatures Great and Small*. At first glance, Skeldale House could be simply a home with four residents, only two of whom are related. There are the Farnon brothers, Siegfried and Tristan, and the housekeeper, Mrs Hall, and employee, James Herriot.

Having travelled with James from his departure at Glasgow to his arrival in Darrowby, we see how the pecking order is established at Skeldale, and it doesn't take too long. Over the first two episodes of series one, the 'family' is created. This fascinating, glorious group of outsiders, all of them strong characters, have made their home in the Yorkshire Dales and in Darrowby and Skeldale.

Siegfried – inspired by Scottish-born Donald Sinclair – is the father figure. Stern, abrupt, impatient, volatile but loveable, the patriarch barks orders and instructions, most of them well intentioned. 'Everyone under this roof is in my care,' says Siegfried at one point. 'Based on what we know of Donald Sinclair,' says Samuel West, who plays Siegfried, 'it follows that Siegfried has to be eccentric, but on the right side of mad.'

Jim Wight says of Donald that 'eccentric is almost too mild a term to describe him but, above all, he was a warm, humorous and interesting person'. Meanwhile Jim's father, writing as James Herriot in the first book, reflects on the initial meeting with Siegfried (and therefore Donald) and describes him as 'just the most English-looking man I had ever seen. Long, humorous, strong-jawed face. Small, clipped moustache, untidy, sandy hair.' He wore an old tweed jacket, shapeless flannel trousers, frayed shirt, carelessly knotted tie. 'He looked', concluded Herriot, 'as though he didn't spend much time in front of a mirror.'

When Herriot meets Siegfried, the latter is in his early thirties. For this adaptation, he is an older man, while Mrs Hall's age is reduced.

Which brings us to the housekeeper heroine of this adaptation. Mrs Hall, the kind-hearted optimist, is cook, cleaner, mother figure and 'a mother with a sixth sense'. She and Siegfried refer to each other in a formal way – he always

'Soon as his pipe's back in his mouth he'll return to normal.'

JAMES TO HELEN, REFERRING TO SIEGFRIED, WHO'S TRYING TO QUIT SMOKING FOR LENT

calls her Mrs Hall, and to her, Siegfried is always Mr Farnon – but they are loyal friends and respect one another. Mind you, every rule must have its exceptions. Early on, when James addresses his employer as Mr Farnon, he is swiftly corrected: 'Siegfried, please. Mr Farnon was my father.'

At times, Mrs Hall is like Siegfried's dutiful wife and mother too, helping him to put on his cufflinks before he goes out for the evening. When he is working too hard, she tells him, 'Bed now!'

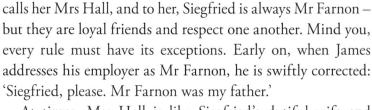

'This calls for a toast. To knowledge, fleas and our growing family.'

SIEGFRIED

She knows where he has left his gloves. When he misplaces his car keys, it is Mrs Hall who hands them to him. Without her, the family ceases to operate, and no, not because she knows where gloves and keys have been left, but because she is the voice of strength, reassurance, resilience and thoughtfulness. In the first episode, when Siegfried seems to be losing his patience with James, she implores him: 'He's a good boy taking his first steps in the working world. You must remember what that were like, how hard it was?' And Siegfried listens.

The depiction and characterization of women is incredibly important in this adaptation of *All Creatures Great and Small*.

'Mrs Hall, I feel you want me to do something but you don't want to ask because once you do, you know I'll have to say yes, and then the illusion that I have at least some semblance of control in the goings on in this place will evaporate, and then where will we be?'

SIEGFRIED

Herriot's books understandably focus on the male characters because they are vets. This series, however, explores more fully the women of the world, ensuring that they have their own stories and agendas. Mrs Hall is brought to life with such meticulous consideration and affection that she becomes one of the most powerful characters of this adaptation.

There we have the parental framework of this 'family' at Skeldale House. Mrs Hall and Mr Farnon are Mam and Dad, albeit with moments of frustration. 'If you have a point, Mrs Hall,' says Siegfried in one episode, 'I'd rather you got on and stabbed me with it.'

What about the 'children', the boys? We like James probably for the same reason that Nicholas Ralph – the actor who plays him – liked James when he first read the scripts before auditioning in 2019. 'He had such compassion and patience,' says Nick of James, 'but he also had a backbone

and would stand up to anyone, especially when it came to the wellbeing of an animal. I really respected and loved that about his character. Little moments like that provided the connection between James and me.' Nick found that he could empathize with the young vet.

Episode two of the first series is entitled 'Another Farnon?' This is the point at which James discovers the answer to the question. Yes, there is another Farnon, and he is very different from his older brother. James collects Tristan from the railway station and from there the brotherly relationship begins – as well as a minor car smash en route back to Skeldale House. There's a bit of chalk and cheese about their relationship. James is dedicated, diligent, conscientious and hardworking. Tristan is the cheeky truant, far happier to be on a sofa reading a *Biggles* adventure, at the breakfast table solving the *Telegraph* crossword or on a stool at the bar of the Drovers' Arms chatting to the barmaid than mixing medicines or stock-taking in the dispensary of the veterinary practice. However, they share the same mischievous sense of humour and they are both targets of Siegfried's irritability, wrath and jibes. As James and Tristan get ready for bed on the night of their meeting, James says, 'You know I don't plan on leaving any time soon.'

Tristan says, 'No one ever does. That's the thing about Siegfried – you never know what he's going to do until he does it. In truth, neither does he. Sleep well.' They will be united in their numerous struggles with Siegfried.

The characters of Siegfried and Tristan Farnon were inspired by the Sinclair brothers, Donald and Brian respectively, Alf's friends and colleagues at 23 Kirkgate. Brian, like Tristan, was an incorrigible prankster. Often he would phone James and – being a brilliant mimic – pretend to be a farmer with a silly or impossible problem that needed sorting out now. In *The Real James Herriot*, Jim Wight refers to Brian's maniacal laugh, which 'began with a low, sinister chuckle before finally ending in wild shrieks of laughter'. After a session in the local pub, 'the streets of Thirsk reverberated with Brian's demented cries'.

Alf Wight, right, with the inspiration for the Farnon brothers, Donald, centre, and Brian Sinclair.

Jim recounts a wonderful story about Brian and a ghost that haunted a stretch of road at Pannal Bank, near Harrogate. The phantom would appear occasionally at the roadside, a shimmering vision of white, and petrified motorists would do a swift U-turn and speed away in the opposite direction. What came to be known as the 'Pannal Ghost' was Brian covered in a large white bedsheet.

One night a couple of motorcyclists were actually not scared. They stopped their motorcycles and gave chase, with Brian scampering off into the darkness, hurrying across fields, illuminated by the glow of his flapping white sheet. He hid in a drainage pipe that was filled with the stench of tom cats, and, writes Jim, it was 'while he was lying in his refuge, with an icy wind screaming down the pipe, that he came to a firm decision: the "Pannal Ghost" would be seen no more'. This was pure nectar for James Herriot, and Jim points out that it inspired the chapter about the 'Raynes Ghost' in *Let Sleeping Vets Lie*.

In Upper Wharfedale, Grassington is the real-life Darrowby; it's the charming village location where the 'family' live and where they shoot those wonderful marketplace scenes for the programme. With its neat square, cobbled streets and cluster of stone shops and houses it seems very much a village in the heart of England's countryside. The Devonshire is snug and cosy with its roaring log fire, or enjoy a pint in the Forester's Arms, and there's always a friendly face in the Stripey Badger bookshop. For supper, an extremely comfortable overnight stay and a hearty breakfast, there's the Gamekeeper's Inn or Grassington House or the Black Horse. Following a morning trek over the fields and hills, the finishing line might be either the Love Brownies café, the Corner Shop Café – serving exceptional fruit scones and toasted tea cakes – or the Retreat Tea Room for a piece of fabulous fruitcake served in the traditional way for this part of the world, with a slice of Wensleydale cheese (in the Wensleydale creamery in Hawes, about 20 miles farther north, they've been making cheese since 1897, and peckish

'I can't be who I am supposed to be if you're always there reminding me of who I'm not.'

TRISTAN TO SIEGFRIED

visitors are welcome). Yes, Grassington is its own hidden-away heaven of tranquillity, hospitality and bonhomie – the picture-postcard village of dales dreams.

Officially, however, Grassington is a town, albeit a small one (population: *c*.1,100), and a market town at that. Granted a charter by Edward I in the thirteenth century, it was thereafter entitled to hold markets and fairs, and it would have been a hub of hustle and bustle, where folk came to sell and buy, mix and mingle, catch up and have fun.

Although sometimes it wasn't much fun. On Main Street there's an old building with a plaque on one of its walls: 'This shop is the original smidy owned by the notorious Tom Lee in the year 1766.' Curious visitors and inquisitive tourists stop at the sign, wonder and ponder. *Smidy? Notorious? Tom Lee? Who was he?* Sit down with a cuppa to hear the grisly tale of Tom …

Once upon a time, Grassington was inhabited by miners who worked in the area's lead mines. A *smidy* was a smithy, or blacksmith's forge, and this one in Main Street was owned by Tom Lee. He was also a publican as well as a highwayman and an all-around tough nut. Villagers lived in fear of him. This cad, bounder, brute and bully, poacher, burglar and robber was known as Black Tom – black as in blacksmith and black as in evil.

His story has been captured in a variety of colourful accounts that have been told over the years. This is one of them.

On 1 April 1766, Tom and a local doctor, Richard Petty, went to a cock fight in Kettlewell, another beautiful village about 6 miles north of Grassington. Tom gambled and lost, while Petty came away with his pockets full of winnings. He would never live long enough to spend and enjoy the cash. Their return journey to Grassington was abruptly halted in Grass Wood, beside the River Wharfe and between Grassington and Conistone. There, Tom stabbed the doctor and stole his money.

Tom Lee was sent for trial at York Assizes but was acquitted due to lack of evidence. There the matter may have ended had it not been for his former apprentice, who came forward with enough evidence to – ahem – nail the blacksmith. Found guilty in 1768, Black Tom was hanged in York, and his body was brought to Grassington to be gibbeted. Still, the story does not end. Black Tom's ghost is said to haunt the cave where he hid, Tom Lee's Cave, and roam the forest. So do watch out for him!

The grim tale has been written about, notably in Victorian times by Joseph Robertshaw under the pseudonym Heather Bell in *Yorkshire Tales and Legends*. The account is delightfully romanticized and unashamedly fictionalized. Here's the bit depicting Black Tom's fate:

> The question was put by the clerk of the court 'Gentlemen of the jury, How find you, is the prisoner at the bar guilty or not guilty?'
>
> 'Guilty, my lord,' was the answer; and the judge assuming the black cap, proceeded at once to pronounce sentence.
>
> Whilst pronouncing the solemn words, a long, loud, piercing shriek rang through the court, alarming every one, and striking terror through the heart of the now doomed Tom Lee; it was his wife, who, no longer supported by hope, on hearing the dreadful words from the lips of the judge, fell senseless into the arms of those about her, and was borne out of court.
>
> The sentence was, that the prisoner was to be hung by the neck till he was dead, and his body gibbeted on the spot where the unnatural and cold-blooded deed had been committed.

Mark Bridgeman's account, *The Grassington Murder* (published in 2023), is a forensic analysis of the notorious crime and a valiant attempt to separate truth from myth, legend and fiction. A very good read it is too. That is a haunting tale of Grassington, but let's return to the happy tales of Herriot and the cheerful life of Darrowby …

'Now you must feel free to avail yourself
of whatever tipple you find in the cellar
– so long as you pour me a glass.'

MRS PUMPHREY TO SIEGFRIED

'Whatever you feel
about sense of duty, just
remember, family comes
first. Always.'

RICHARD ALDERSON

All Creatures Great and Small is not merely about a family. The books by Herriot and the TV series are the embodiment of a sense of family. The BBC series of *All Creatures* was first broadcast in 1978, and it ran for seven series and ninety episodes until 1990. The show had a fantastic cast: Christopher Timothy as James, Robert Hardy as Siegfried, Peter Davison as Tristan, Carol Drinkwater and then the late Lynda Bellingham as Helen. Mary Hignett played Mrs Hall in the early days, but she died after the filming of the third series. (In the BBC series, incidentally, Mrs Hall's first name was Edna and not Audrey.)

Families gathered around the television to watch. At its launch there were only three TV stations, BBC1, BBC2 and ITV. It would be another four years before Channel 4 was launched in 1982, and Channel 5 was born in 1997. *All Creatures Great and Small* appealed to all ages, young and old. Indeed, the millions who were glued to their screens included a few who would go on to play an instrumental role in the production of the hugely popular series of the same name that we enjoy watching today.

Brian Percival was one of them and is one of the directors of the current adaptation. Sir Colin Callender – the CEO of Playground, the production company behind the series – was another. He remembers how it made him feel when the idea for this new version came along. 'I thought we could bring this back to life,' says Sir Colin, 'and entertain in the way that the BBC series had done, but for a contemporary audience.'

Nicholas Ralph with director Brian Percival.

Left to right: actor Cat Simmons as Grace Chapman, director Stewart Svaasand and actor Cleo Sylvestre as Anne Chapman.

Ben Vanstone was appointed lead writer of the show for series one to three. As a lad, he'd sit enchanted as he watched the BBC's adaptation of *All Creatures*. 'I suppose it was one of the first shows that I remember as a kid,' he recalls. 'Watching with my family on a Sunday night.'

The producers' self-set mission was to replicate and deliver the warmth, humour and poignancy of Herriot's books, as well as the same feeling that the BBC series evoked. 'We had to deliver the same experience,' says Melissa – nostalgic but with a contemporary approach to storytelling. 'We wanted to explore Herriot's characters in greater depth, in a way that would sit respectfully alongside our predecessors. It had to be confidently new without turning its back on the things

The cast and crew for series four.

people loved about *All Creatures*. If the audience didn't come back for the world and the characters, then we'd have got it wrong.'

Jackie Smith, the production designer (and therefore creator of the brilliant set for Skeldale House), is a Yorkshire lass. As a child, Jackie immersed herself in the Herriot memoirs, and she was a fan of the BBC show. Samuel West, too, enjoyed the

series and loved the books. Although Rachel Shenton hadn't seen the first series – 'it was a bit before my time' – her mum was ecstatic when Rachel landed a key role in this show.

Jill Clark, who, with her son Dean, trains the animals for the show, describes herself as 'a devoted fan' of Herriot. 'I read all of the books, and years ago I was one of the millions who watched the series. What really appeals to me is the compassion James Herriot showed towards the animals he was working with. He was down-to-earth and, in fact, similar to my own vet.' And Mark Atkinson, who, with his son Ben, trains the horses for the show, is also a huge fan of Herriot and has read all the books. 'Going back to the mid-1970s, I was a member of a young farmers' club and we'd do competitions in public speaking and prose,' says Mark. 'I won the junior public speaking prose competition when I read from James Herriot's *Vet in Harness*.' Mark's daughter, Lucy, did some work experience at the museum, the World of James Herriot, 'and loved it'.

The members of the ensemble cast and crew see their relationship as being like a family; away from the set, they and the entire cast and crew is an even bigger family making a show about the family in Skeldale House. And the show is as much for families now as the series was in the late 1970s, when it first came into the living rooms of Britain.

Then there is the family of Alf Wight, his children Jim and Rosie and their families. They are a part of the production, sharing insight that has been valuable to the writers, the cast and the producers. At the first meeting with the members of the ensemble cast, Jim gave a copy of his biography, *The Real James Herriot*, to each of them – an especially helpful guide for the actors as they prepared for their roles. Jim reads the scripts in advance so he can offer advice and spot howlers. He also recommended the on-set vet, Andy Barrett, who worked with Jim and his father as well as Donald and Brian at 23 Kirkgate. (Andy is also a stand-in for Nick – when you see a close-up of Nick's hands during a difficult procedure they belong to Andy.)

In Herriot's books, we see Helen through the eyes of James and how he felt about her, but we don't see life from her perspective. The story within the series needed to appeal to a modern-day audience, with well-rounded, multifaceted, strong female characters. 'And while there is a limited amount of material in the books,' says Rachel, 'we do know that Helen is based on Alf Wight's wife, Joan. We were super fortunate to be able to talk to Rosie and Jim. Through them I gained an insight; they were just short anecdotes, but they left me feeling as if I'd peeped behind the curtain. I could understand Helen. Rosie said that if there was ever going to be a cheeky joke in the house, it'd always be Joan who told it.

'There is no better test of a man's character than how he gets along with a dog.'

GEORGE PANDHI

That sort of anecdote is really helpful because it brings Helen alive for me.'

Often the animals are also members of the family. Being a veterinary practice, Skeldale frequently has animals for a sleepover, but the four-legged residents are Jess – Mrs Hall and Jess have long chats when they're alone together in the kitchen – and the abandoned Springer Spaniel Dash. Oh, and Siegfried's pet rat and office companion, Vonolel.

For the farmers of the 1930s, livestock equalled livelihood. Cattle, sheep and poultry were a source of income, and the death of one cow led to diminishing profits. Widow Phyllis Dalby (played by Amy Nuttall) has her cattle herd saved twice

in one year by James. She tells his parents: 'If it weren't for your lad, we'd not have a roof over our head.' Think of farmer Kate Billings, played by Lynda Rooke, who (in episode two of the third series) calls in Siegfried after the mysterious death of one of her calves. She is beside herself with worry that another one will die. 'These calves,' Kate says. 'They're like family to me … They're all I've got left.'

In series three, episode five, Mr Sunningwell (Ian Mercer) rushes into the practice with Benjamin, the sheepdog who's been kicked by a horse. 'He's all I've got. It's just me and him. He's the only living, breathing thing I've got left connecting me to her [his mother].' While Mr Dakin (James Bolam), the livestock farmer, watches sadly as his cow, Blossom, is about to be put on a truck and taken to the slaughterhouse: 'Goodbye, old girl. Come on, then. I remember the night she was born. Snow coming down hard. I put a sack over her to keep her warm. I picked her up, helped her stand. She never made a fuss. She's always been a gentle soul, has Blossom.' Thankfully, Siegfried sees a way of saving Blossom.

'One minute the house is full of folk and laughter, the next it's empty.'

RECENTLY WIDOWED FARMER CLIFFORD SLAVENS

'He can't even raise a paw – I've not been able to convince him to eat a single thing for three days now. Cook's tried all sorts – toad in the hole, suet and beef.'

MRS PUMPHREY
GIVING SIEGFRIED
AN ACCOUNT OF
TRICKI'S ILL-HEALTH

And then there's Tricki, Mrs Pumphrey's beloved Pekingese, who is terribly spoiled and feasts on a diet of cake and chicken, with occasional treats of caviar, smoked kippers and trifle from Fortnum & Mason. In *If Only They Could Talk*, Mrs Pumphrey describes Tricki as 'an only dog', like an only child. When she collects Tricki after his stay at Skeldale, Mrs Pumphrey takes the dog in her arms and groans. 'My goodness, he feels like a sack of spanners. He must be starving.' Richard Carmody finds it all very strange, but as James tells him: 'Imagine her pets are her children. Then her behaviour don't seem so strange … I know it doesn't come easily to you, but next time try and pay Tricki special attention. She's an important client and I need her to trust you. Please.'

Tricki is played by Derek, who is a natural and regarded as 'a real pro' by Patricia Hodge, who plays Mrs Pumphrey. Derek is, she says, 'very, very sweet-natured. Pick him up and tickle his tummy and he purrs like a giant cat.' Nicholas Ralph is adamant: 'You're never going to win a scene when Derek's in it.' Derek's owner is Jill Clark, who says that, just like the character he plays on screen, Derek is extremely spoiled. He might not be on a diet of Fortnum's goodies, but Derek does have his own special gadgets and luxuries. 'He has a big hairdryer – it's like a leaf blower – which I use after he's had a bath,' says Jill. 'It gets out the undercoat and dries him very quickly. He also has his own little leather sofa. But that's how it should be – he's such a sweetheart.'

LOVE AND ROMANCE

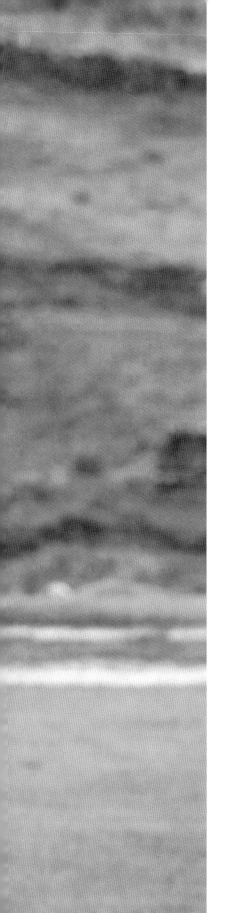

Just as love was in the Yorkshire air for Alf Wight, his creation James Herriot finds it here too. For Alf, it was as a young vet in Thirsk that he met Joan, the woman he would marry and with whom he would have two children, Jim and Rosie. In *All Creatures Great and Small*, the dales provides the setting for James's first encounter with Helen Alderson, the character inspired by Joan.

James and Helen meet on the bus to Darrowby, but, as we will see, their journey together develops into far more than simply a trip on a juddering red charabanc through the heart of the Yorkshire countryside. The relationship between James and Helen is an adventure that remains the focus of attention from one episode to the next – oh, how we want them to be together and happy and married! Be patient; they shall be all of these.

What of the other residents of Darrowby and especially of Skeldale House, the veterinary practice? What is romantically in store for Siegfried, the widower, and his young brother Tristan, the fun flirt who struggles to be taken seriously? Will Eros, the Greek god of love, find an arrow for Mrs Hall, the housekeeper with the hugest heart but burdened by the darkest memories of a failed marriage? In a world recovering from one great war and heading for another, the folk of the dales search for companionship and this is crucial – fun. We may not have lived through a world war, but we all experienced the Covid pandemic, and how often was love the thing that saw us through?

'Helen – I fell in love with a woman who drags
bulls around a yard. I don't want to change
who you are. I wouldn't want to change a thing
about you.'

JAMES

It is 1937, two years before the outbreak of the Second World War, when James and Helen meet. He is a young vet, born and raised near the docks of Glasgow. If he hadn't persisted with his passion to be a veterinary surgeon, James would probably have been working in the docks as an apprentice plater. He is a vulnerable, good-humoured chap, eager to please and, as Helen later says of him, selfless. She is a farmer's daughter, but, following the death of her mother, she has adopted the role of farmhouse matriarch and mother to her younger sister, Jenny. When the actress Rachel Shenton thinks of the character she plays, she is reminded of her own grandmother's words: 'Men moan. Babies cry. Women cope.' Helen Alderson is very much the woman who copes, out on the farm or in the kitchen, cleaning the farmhouse and cooking the meals for her father and sister – although she's not the domestic goddess of the dales and is prone to burning cakes and toast. (As for her voice, it has become second nature to actress Rachel, who says, 'It's that lovely warm, thick Yorkshire accent, and I can't help but take it on a bit.')

Helen and James cannot embark instantly on a relationship. These things take time, and, after all, Darrowby does not do clear-cut, simple and straightforward. The course of true love never did run smooth, and for James there is one major obstacle: Helen has another suitor. Hugh Hulton is a wealthy and at times kind landowner … and soon, much to James's disappointment, Helen accepts Hugh's marriage proposal. They will be married on Christmas Day.

Or at least, that is the plan. Hugh pops along to a Christmas Eve party at Skeldale House but doesn't stay long, as he's off to meet a few chums at the Renniston ('last night of freedom and all that'). As he leaves, he says to Helen: 'I guess I'll see you at the church.'

Helen smiles. 'This time tomorrow we'll be married,' she says.

'I know,' says Hugh. 'And then the rest of our lives.' They grin at each other, kiss again and then break apart, with Hugh disappearing into the night, the man heading off to toast the rest of his life but unaware that it's a life that he'll not spend with Helen.

'I thought since it's Friday we could listen to Once a Week on the Home Service. Have a seat and I'll be right with you.'

GERALD HAMMOND
TO MRS HALL

Rachel Shenton has often thought about what she would have asked Joan Wight if she could have met her. 'I'd ask about the relationship between her and Alf. I've heard it from the perspective of Jim and Rosie. They talked to me with such fondness about their mum and dad's relationship, and I almost feel like I've been let into some kind of secret love story. I know they were totally devoted to each other and that they never had a cross word. They had each other's backs through everything, standing up for each other. Their strengths and weaknesses complement each other. I'd like to ask her, "Was it all as good as it seemed?"'

So often love stories involve a clichéd setting such as the terrace of a bustling sunlit café in Paris (cue accordion music) within the shadow of the Eiffel Tower, or a moonlit moment beside the Trevi Fountain in Rome with wishes being made and coins being tossed into the water. Some classics of romantic literature, however, do take the reader on an adventure to the north of England.

The Brontë sisters, Charlotte, Emily and Anne, set their novels in West Yorkshire, where they lived. Think of Emily's *Wuthering Heights*, with Heathcliff, dirty, dark-haired, brooding and sullen, and Catherine, beautiful but temperamental, on the windswept heathered moors, while in Charlotte's *Jane Eyre*, Jane falls in love with Rochester amid the fields, glens and sometimes rocky landscape around Thornfield. These novelist sisters used landscape as a device to illustrate perhaps the mood of a particular character or the drama of a certain scene. Weather is also woven into the narrative by novelists as a way to help paint the necessary picture of that moment in time. The heartbreak of a hero or heroine is accompanied by thunder and lightning, while a moment of joy or elation tends to come when the sun is shining and birds are chirruping in the trees. Our vets of the dales are out in all weathers. In episode one of the first series, James and Siegfried are driving along and the former takes in the wonderful views. 'It's marvellous,' says James.

Siegfried tuts. 'You won't be saying that when the snow's 8 foot deep. I've known this pass to be blocked for weeks on end.' James promises to keep a shovel with him.

The great Romantic poet William Wordsworth also worshipped nature and, with quill pen in hand and before him the landscape of England's Lake District, brought into his poems and ballads boisterous brooks, green valleys and vales, tall rocks and deep and gloomy woods. Wordsworth viewed nature almost as a living being. 'His heart is enriched in the company of nature and he does not want to leave its company.' That is how one critic has described the poet's strong connection to nature. The story he told within a ballad featured nature because it was inseparable from his view of life and the view in front of him.

Samuel West, who plays Siegfried, also sees *All Creatures* as 'a story that's about living in harmony with nature'. Nicholas Ralph remembers travelling by train through the dales, taken aback by the landscape's scale of beauty. As he peered through the window, he thought, *This is insane – it's like a painting.*

The rolling dales were scattered with sheep and strewn with dry-stone walls, and there was the occasional solitary silhouette of a tree on the peak of a dale. Similarly, Herriot writes of being struck by the wonderful views that greeted him when he arrived in this part of England. Melissa Gallant, executive producer, says of making the show: 'You can do all the planning you like, but nature is in charge.' Nature is not only a hindrance but also a help. In the first episode, as James gets off the bus, he takes in the view of miles of green land and hills and then in a split second his hat is suddenly blown from his head. That wasn't planned. A gust of wind blew his hat away, and the moment was captured, as was the sudden appearance of the sun. 'The Yorkshire gods came out for us,' says Erik Molberg Hansen, the Danish-born director of photography.

Sir Colin Callender talks about the very early stages when he considered the show and why it could be different from the BBC series because of how modern technology would enable the dales nature to be portrayed. 'New digital technology would allow us to shoot everything in a way in which the landscape and the world of the Yorkshire Dales could be brought to life in a very beautiful way.' (This time around, with this adaptation, we get to see the dales in all their majestic glory thanks to drones and modern technology.)

Director Brian Percival recalls driving through the dales, and this was before he had even discussed the project with Sir Colin. Brian stopped the car, got out and looked at the valley that stretched out before him. A keen landscape photographer, he experienced not only a eureka moment but a sort of Wordsworth moment too. Brian saw the dales as an ever-developing character within the series. Sure, nature is in charge, but Brian says, 'You just have to accept that beauty comes in different forms. It can't always be with sunshine. Sometimes you look at the moors covered with mist and it's pouring with rain and it's stunning. But it's a different sort of beauty. That's the whole thing about landscapes – part of it stays the same, but much of it changes. It's all about embracing that.'

Now, Thirsk – the main inspiration for Darrowby – is about 100 miles east of Cockermouth, where Wordsworth lived. And Thirsk is about 50 miles north-west of the parsonage where the Brontë sisters lived and wrote in the mid-1800s. We're in a different part of northern England, but still nature plays a leading role, from the hills and the brooks and streams to the green valleys and vales, the wind, rain and sunshine.

Love story or not, any major development in the human plot requires animals if at all possible. We are in the sweeping hills of the North Yorkshire countryside, where the closest thing to a Parisian café is the Drovers' Arms and the nearest thing to the Trevi Fountain is the pond in the grounds of Mrs Pumphrey's mansion. And so a dramatic twist – the *coup de théâtre* – in James and Helen's relationship comes on Christmas Eve and involves the birth of Border Collie pups in the Christmas episode of the first series. Moments after Hugh's departure there's a telephone call to Skeldale House. 'Hello, Darrowby 2297 ...' Bert and Anne Chapman's sheepdog Suzie is having trouble giving birth at their cottage high in the dales. James is about to leave the party and head to Suzie's rescue when Helen – who is tired of being interrogated by other guests about the wedding – asks if she can join him: 'Please, James. Anything to take my mind off it all.' Together they drive to the Chapmans' smallholding and, in the cottage, James sets to work, watched not only by Helen but also by Bert (Dave Hill) and his wife, Anne (played by Cleo Sylvestre, who was, incidentally, the first black woman to play a lead role at the National Theatre in London).

Helen observes admiringly. 'Place your hand here,' says James, and he takes Helen's hand and places it on Suzie's flank. 'Keep stroking her. Try to keep her calm.' The birth is a moment of tension, as the first puppy, a boy, doesn't appear to be breathing and Anne asks if he is dead. James blows into the pup's mouth, trying to get some air into his lungs, and then he lays him down in the basket beside Suzie: 'Let's see if his mother can get him going.' Which Suzie does, and the delivery of the pups has the happiest of endings. Throughout, Helen has watched James, the kind, caring and gifted veterinary surgeon. She is in love with James ... but tomorrow she is due to walk down the aisle to marry another man. With its naturalness, this scene is a metaphor for rebirth.

Mother Nature assists again, sending a thick blanket of fog that sets in and prevents James and Helen from driving back to Skeldale House. They'll have to stay until morning, when the fog will lift.

Anne Chapman is reminded of meeting Bert many years ago. She says there 'weren't many around here who wanted to see a Yorkshireman marry a woman that looked like me. But you can't help who you fall in love with ... Both of us tried to fight it. We knew it'd cost us our jobs, our friends. It were worse for Bert, of course. I was already an outsider. By rights Bert should've wanted nowt to do with me. But love don't see with the eyes. It comes from in here. In the end, there's no fighting it.'

Who can argue with that? Helen glances at James. She knows what we know. It's love. 'Where do you get your water?' she asks Anne. 'I'll put us a brew on.' All of this is heading (at a pace now) in one direction. There's only one loser and his name is Hugh Hulton.

It's the next day, the big day. James is at the wheel of Siegfried's Rover, driving home for Christmas in Glasgow with his parents, and he's a few miles from Darrowby. From a kestrel's-eye view we see him stop at the crossroads – the same one where he stopped for a moment when he first arrived in the dales and stepped from the bus after meeting Helen. The crossroads of his life. Should he continue on his way or should he turn the car around and return to Darrowby and to Helen? He chooses the latter – thank heavens! Something inside him says he should be at the church. And life, as Helen had told him the previous night at the Chapmans' cottage, 'has a funny way about it sometimes'.

Pulling up outside the church where the nuptials are due to have taken place, James sees Tristan. 'Have I missed it?' asks James.

Tristan replies, 'Oh, did you ever.'

Inside, Helen is on a pew at the front of the church. James sits with her. 'Oh, James. What have I done?' She breaks down in tears, and he puts an arm around her and holds her close. 'Let's get you home,' he says. For the briefest of moments they are there, at the altar, hand in hand, and, in an otherwise empty church, they turn and walk down the aisle together, James Herriot and Helen Alderson … What follows in the second series is the romance, slowly blossoming, between James and Helen, gently leading towards that day when they will walk down the aisle as Mr and Mrs Herriot. And still we have to wait slightly longer, as that day comes in episode one of the third series.

Predictably, their impending nuptials and the honeymoon are bothersome for Siegfried – it's one less man at the practice. They're all in the dining room and about to eat a feast when he raises the subject. 'You know, James,' says Siegfried, 'this wedding business is really rather inconsiderate of you.'

'Oh, is it, Siegfried?' says Helen.

'Yes, it damned well is,' Siegfried continues. 'And then there's the honeymoon you're drifting gaily off on.'

Tristan chips in. 'A week in North Riding. Lovely.'

'It's not lovely,' says Siegfried. 'It's bloody awful. A whole week! And I'm here, running around and disappearing halfway up my own backside!'

'Only halfway,' says Helen. 'Should have booked in for two.'

IN SEARCH OF LOVE

While Tristan is the champion flirt, Siegfried wonders
if anyone can ever replace his late wife, Evelyn.

SIEGFRIED

A young James Herriot is perplexed by the romantic lives
of the Farnon brothers. Herriot writes of streams of female
visitors to Skeldale House. Done up to the nines, they come
to swoon over Siegfried. The most ardent (and determined)
admirer is Diana Brompton, who is played by Dorothy
Atkinson (also known for her performance in *Mum*). Herriot
writes of meeting Diana at Skeldale House before he met
Siegfried, but she was dismissive of the young vet. She's fun
and flirty, foxtrots with Siegfried and even has advice for
Mrs Hall to woo Gerald Hammond: 'A little feeling makes
you feel a whole lot.' He is on pins all day knowing that she
is coming for dinner, and when Helen asks Mrs Hall how
she swung an invitation, the latter responds: 'My guess is she
talked him into it. She's nothing if not persistent.' Siegfried is
also very taken by Mrs Hall's friend from the Wrens, Dorothy
(Maimie McCoy). 'Oh, hello there,' are his opening words
when he sees her at the surgery, and it goes from there but
doesn't quite develop before she has to return to Malta.

'I think you're a
very fortunate man,
Mr Farnon. You've built
a life doing what you love
most. Not many people
manage that.'

DOROTHY

TRISTAN

'Bone idle' Tristan, meanwhile, intrigues James because he seems to regard the nurses' home as an agency to supply him with female company. 'I won't have a man under my roof mess a girl around,' Mrs Hall tells Tris. 'You're better than that, Tristan.'

'Yes, Mrs H,' he promises, but can he stop himself? He seems to adore Maggie, the barmaid at the Drovers' Arms. He invites a couple of nurses, Connie and Brenda, to a gathering at Skeldale House ('Lovely girls,' he tells James. 'Bright, witty, wonderful bedside manner …'). For a time he is enchanted by farmer's daughter Anabel Dinsdale (Ella Bruccoleri). And he is fascinated by Margot Sebright Saunders (Jessica Clark), though she is destined for a relationship with Hugh Hulton. Is Tristan holding out for Mrs Right? 'There've certainly been plenty of Mrs Wrongs,' says Siegfried. Is he simply good company and a laugh but a terrible prospect as a husband? This question worries him.

'You're like a magpie, flitting from one shiny object to the next. All the girls know it, and are happy to have fun with you, while it is still fun.'

MAGGIE TO TRISTAN

Then he meets Florence, daughter of Siegfried's rival, George Pandhi, and played by Sophie Khan Levy, below. Tristan takes Florence for a drive, adding that he's free most of the coming month 'or even this year'. They picnic on top of a rock, overlooking treetops and the rolling hills beyond – 'The only person holding you back is you, Tristan Farnon.' He proposes but, alas, Florence declines.

'Sometimes we need to stare that monster right in the eye. Show it we're not afraid of it any more.'

SIEGFRIED TO MRS HALL AS SHE DELIBERATES FILLING IN FORMS FOR DIVORCE

Meanwhile, we are all rooting for Mrs Hall to find a mister who can help her rebuild her life. In Herriot's books she is not much more than a figure of grim benevolence who welcomes James when he first knocks on the door of Skeldale House. Surrounded by her servile pack of five dogs, she then disappears down the hallway into the back of the house. Afterwards she is firmly in the scullery, barely seen, rarely heard.

However, in this television adaptation, Mrs Hall is a central figure. Indeed, she is the beating heart of the 'family' that lives in Skeldale House. Sir Colin Callender sees her as 'an emotional pivot. These three guys – Siegfried, Tristan, James – are flailing and running in opposite directions. Mrs Hall keeps them all grounded and honest.' She also has a first name – Audrey, or Aud as she is known to some, though she is often called Mrs H by Tristan. We are gradually drip-fed morsels about her past, so that little by little we learn about the life of Mrs Hall, who comes from another part of Yorkshire. She was married to Robert, who fought in the Great War, and they have a son, Edward. Robert returned from the war, hit the bottle and turned into 'a brute'. Edward stole from his mother's previous employer. She writes to Edward and sends him gifts but does not hear from him.

She is strong (both physically and emotionally), resilient and never off duty. Women of the 1930s worked as hard as the men, and keeping the house was a thoroughly demanding job, with early starts and late finishes. The next time you hit the start button on your washing machine or tumble dryer, spare a thought for Mrs Hall and the housekeepers and housewives of the thirties and the laborious process of cleaning clothes: washing by hand with soap suds, passing the wet clothes through a mangle to rinse out excess water, hanging the clothes on the line to dry. Veterinary coats, sullied and stained, were an extra challenge. (If you own vintage clothes with broken buttons, blame the mangle they were once pushed through.)

Often, she delivers dialogue while in her apron and tackling one chore or another – serving breakfast, rolling pastry, removing a tray of scones from the oven, hanging out

the washing, ironing, cleaning the house, cleaning the silver, shopping, in the pantry making pickles and jam, waving her carpet-beater as she beats the dust out of a rug, cutting freshly baked shortbread, carrying trays heaving with food and tea things, rushing to answer the knocking door, darting to answer the ringing phone and, of course, frequently getting a brew on for the many visitors to Skeldale.

So surely Mrs Hall really does deserve a break in life, doesn't she? Knock, knock. Enter Mr Hammond (played by Will Thorp) with his injured dog, Rock, seeking veterinary help. Gerald Hammond is a kind soul, introverted, thoughtful and well-meaning. He is happy on his allotment. He is a fixer. He fixes Skeldale's grandfather clock so that it keeps good time and, later on, he mends the pipe under the kitchen sink. But, we wonder, can he soothe the sorrow in Mrs Hall's life? Can he help ease her heartbreak when she thinks about her absent son, Edward?

'I never imagined when you get to our age,' Gerald says to Audrey, and leaves a pause. 'You never think you might meet someone who changes your life the way you have mine … I always hoped …' But, after the dramatic tension, he tells Mrs Hall that he intends to be with his unwell sister in the Lake District. 'You'll be back, though,' says Audrey. 'I don't know.'

Anna Madeley says of Mrs Hall, the character she plays: 'She has found a good place to be, is valued, has fun and she has the community around her. She is aware of her own identity, her self-worth, and I think there is something appealing about her degree of independence. And this spurred something in series two – whether she might entertain meeting someone new, contemplate the possibilities of opening up her heart again, live a full life.'

As the relationship develops between Audrey and Gerald, their dogs also become more attached. They go for walks and enjoy picnics beside the stream in episode four of the third series. However, Mrs Hall is timid, hesitant about embarking on another relationship. Why? She is a decent church-going woman with a strong faith. Mrs Hall still holds sacred her marriage vows as she is not yet divorced.

HANNAH HAUXWELL

It is the early 1970s and a middle-aged woman packs her bag, says farewell to her sheepdog, closes the front door of her farmhouse in the north Yorkshire Dales and sets off on a journey 250 miles south to London. So far there is nothing exceptional. After all, how many women must make this journey every single week?

Yet this was Hannah Hauxwell. A woman in her forties, she lived alone on the desperately remote Low Birk Hatt Farm. She had never been to London. She rarely left Baldersdale, the Dale in which she lived. Weeks passed without her seeing another soul. Her home had no electricity. She also existed without running water and washed her clothes in the reservoir beside her 80-acre holding. Hannah lived on 5 pounds a week, and once a month she trudged across fields to collect a package of food that was left for her in a milk churn. She was like Herriot – there wasn't a blizzard or torrential downpour that could stop her from working. It seems that Herriot, without question, would have made a few chapters at least out of Hannah, although they were separated by a drive of at least an hour (in good weather conditions).

Hannah Hauxwell's name might mean nothing to you, and perhaps she would have remained virtually unknown. However, one day in 1973, a film crew from Yorkshire Television descended on the dales to make a documentary, *Too Long a Winter*. The programme centred on farmers as they struggled with the tough conditions of a harsh – to us, but to them quite normal – winter in the High Pennines. Hannah was one of those farmers who was filmed as she went about her chores while a storm of snow raged around her. The crew found the bleak conditions almost unbearable. She was described as 'the most materially deprived person' in the country.

'It must get lonely, out here on your own.'

JAMES TO FARMER
KATE BILLINGS

When the documentary was broadcast, the sight of poor Hannah wrenched the heart of a nation. Almost overnight she became an adored celebrity. One of the compelling qualities of Hannah was that she was entirely happy with her lot. She neither moaned about the weather nor grumbled about finances or having to wash her clothes in the reservoir. She was softly spoken, humble. On her favourite walk, she said, she'd often stop and look around at the landscape, the countryside, and think, *If I haven't money in my pocket, it's one thing nobody can rob me of. It's mine. It's mine for the taking.*

The main characters of Herriot's stories have a part of Hannah in them: the resolute resilience of James; Siegfried's stiff upper lip; Tristan's unconquerable optimism; Helen's strong work ethic; Mrs Hall's hopefulness that it will all work out well in the end. Hannah was all of these things and a symbol of hope and inspiration. Her tender, sweet story was poignant and compelling. Viewers sent money to help her out, and she bought more cows for her farm.

Hannah was invited to the Woman of the Year lunch at the Savoy, and this would be the journey that took her away from home and to London. It was a home built by her ancestors, where she had lived since the age of three, and a holding she had farmed since the death of her uncle in 1961. She was put up in a sumptuous suite at the hotel, all expenses paid. This would become another documentary, *Hannah Goes to Town*. A camera crew, directed by Barry Cockcroft, who had made the earlier documentary, followed and filmed her as she took a stroll through the capital, mesmerized by the bustling streets, the bright lights and a trip on the Tube.

In Yorkshire, she had bought a dress for the occasion. Hannah was very much a make-do-and-mend woman, just like Mrs Hall and Helen. This was the first dress she had bought in eighteen years, and 'the biggest price I paid for a dress was four pounds'.

She was excited about just catching a glimpse of another woman at the lunch – the heroic Odette Hallowes, the French Resistance spy who had survived Nazi imprisonment

'On a clear day you can see for 20 miles. But when the weather comes in, it's a brutal place. Snow 10 foot deep. Fog so thick you can't see your hand in front of your face.'

JAMES

and interrogation during the Second World War. Indeed, it was Odette who came up to Hannah, telling her how much she admired her. 'Thank you,' said Hannah, and she was blessed with good manners too, forever polite. 'It's very kind … No, thank you … Yes, please. Thank you.'

Barry Cockcroft wondered if she could swap what could be seen as loneliness in the countryside for companionship in the capital. Hannah was having none of it. A dales farmer, she was not easily swayed, as Helen would say. Hannah was, remember, a woman nurtured by nature. She would go on to travel around Europe and the States with Cockcroft and his cameras following.

'If one is rather short on things in life in the country you can go out and there's the hills and the river, the streams, in summertime the birds singing,' said Hannah. 'They don't fail you. I'm sure you could be much more lonely in London than in the country.' She paused, smiled and added softly but firmly: 'I have my shaggy dog. He's a little rascal but he's wonderful company.' You can sense a knowing nod from Herriot, who was 'beguiled' by the charms of the Yorkshire countryside and, as we all know, absolutely adored his dogs.

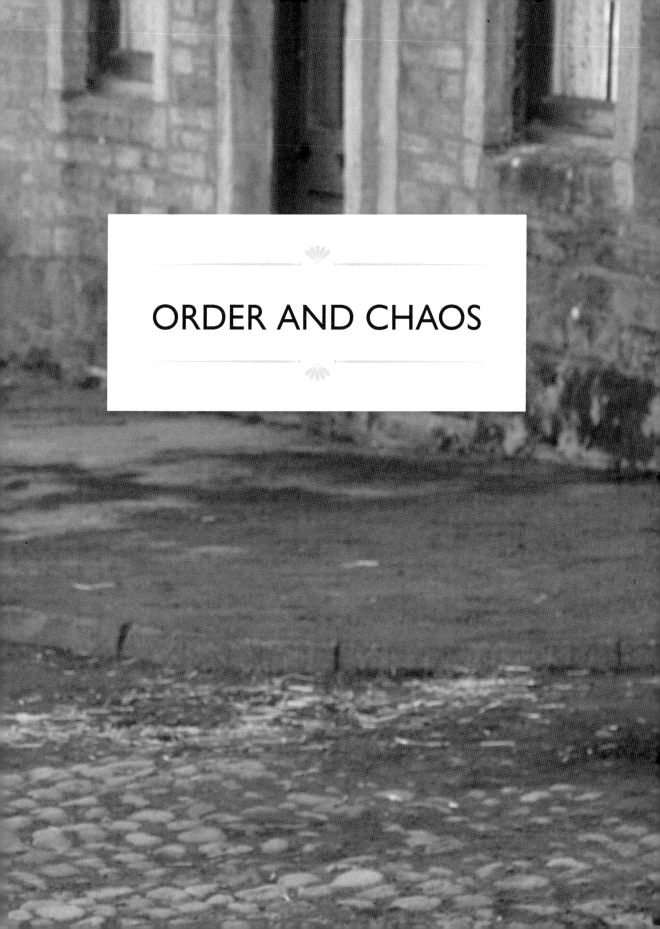

ORDER AND CHAOS

There is no doubt that *All Creatures Great and Small* is a seesaw. Order is at one end and chaos at the other, and it goes up and down continuously. And that's a big part of the joy of this show. What is already fixed is broken … and then fixed and perhaps broken again. In May 2019, four months before filming began, the 'series bible' was circulated. It was a well-considered, well-crafted map of how the writers and producers saw the characters and the development of the story from one episode to the next.

Of course, everything can change. In fact, the bible refers to Helen holding up the family, 'raising her younger siblings, William and Mabel'. One storyline saw William skipping school and hiding out in the shed at Skeldale House. In the process of creativity, William was eliminated as a character – Helen does not have a brother in the series. And Mabel was renamed Jenny (played by Imogen Clawson). Helen was given a sister in this adaptation because it was felt interesting to have two female siblings on a farm with no boys to inherit it and a Yorkshire farmer (Richard Alderson) bringing up two girls. Helen and Jenny also mirror Siegfired and Tristan; an older sibling being a surrogate parent to a younger sibling. Alf Wight would have understood. In his early attempts at semi-autobiographical novels, Siegfried and Tristan Farnon had the surname Vernon. Their first names derive, Herriot explains, from their father's love of German composer Richard Wagner, whose operas included *Tristan und Isolde*, and his son was called Siegfried.

This draft of the bible, however, is an indication of where the show is heading, and it was distributed among the crew and cast. The bible – dated 30 May 2019 – was a fundamental guide for the actors and the producers and for the production's key figures such as director Brian Percival, production designer Jackie Smith, costume designer Ros Little, and Lisa Parkinson, the hair and makeup designer. This was a series sat-nav, with format and story outlines, and it helped to guide everyone from A to Z, or rather gave a synopsis of plots that would eventually be presented, from the opening lines to the end credits of a fifty-five-page script (cue Alexandra Harwood's theme tune).

The bible's early draft is a testament to the careful planning of chaos. A portrait of Tristan, for instance, is painted like this:

> A bon vivant whose spirit refuses to be crushed, Tristan (20s) is very fond of a pint and considers himself something of an expert on women. He is more interested in having fun than working hard. He's not driven to be a vet and his love of a pint of beer masks a sense of inferiority that he can't live up to his older brother's expectations for him. Qualifying as a vet would mean Siegfried would have one less reason to shout at him but it could also reveal how he would fall short of his older brother's accomplishments. His frequent drunken antics, his pranks and haphazard work ethic land him, and the practice, in frequent trouble.

Tristan 'brings a vital energy … and is a constant source of comedy and chaos which we will love him for'.

In Herriot's books, Siegfried is a bachelor. However, Ben Vanstone and the producers wanted him to be a widower like the real Siegfried, Donald Sinclair, whose first wife, as previously mentioned, died from tuberculosis when Donald was in his twenties. (Sadly, Alf had also lost a girlfriend to the disease.) Siegfried's story is that his wife Evelyn died four years ago from cancer. 'Not only was she a great support to Siegfried in his parenting of Tristan, she was also his right hand at the surgery. She ran the bookings, charmed the clients, prepped his surgeries and knew exactly how much cat gut he would need for stitching.' And so Siegfried's reluctance to hire a veterinary assistant 'has not just stemmed from his own brand of chaos but from the fact that Evelyn Farnon was irreplaceable'.

The bible included the format of the show, in which it described Skeldale House as 'a place of warmth, love and fun,

as well as a place of chaos'. The bible adds: 'The family stories will often provide comic relief as our eclectic mix of characters rub up against one another. The dynamic in Skeldale House will also be impacted by and feed into what's going on professionally in James's life and will provide real emotional stakes. Cases will sometimes involve all three of our vets and on surgery days, Mrs Hall may be embroiled too, when chaos from the practice spills over into her domestic realm.'

And speaking of domesticity, chaos is reflected in the set of Skeldale House. Siegfried's office was not a feature of Herriot's books, but in this series Jackie Smith and Brian Percival decided to give him his own private space, along with his wife's music room. These rooms provide an insight into Siegfried's past, with photographs of his late wife. They are also a reflection of the chaos of his mind – with paperwork, bills and invoices strewn across his desk.

'Whatever you've heard, it's not true.
I didn't do it.'

TRISTAN

Jackie Smith found some original wallpaper from the 1930s that was perfect for the walls of the scullery. 'The pattern brought to mind dry-stone walls and has a floral motif,' she says. 'To me, it was a metaphor for what we were trying to achieve – an underlying structure of strength and grit, but with a kind of layer of chaos over it. This could be seen metaphorically in terms of the grit shown by the characters in the story and the chaos coming from the everyday dramas they encounter, and also literally, as it references the landscape.' This wasn't simply old wallpaper but symbolic. 'It summed up what I was trying to achieve with the set and really the whole show. It portrays how nature disregards our attempts to try to organize it.'

MAKING MAYHEM

Chaos unfolds in the first series, as we can see from these highlights of madness, confusion and pandemonium in episodes one to five. All extracts taken from 'the bible'.

'WE'VE GOT TO DREAM'
BY BEN VANSTONE

James leaves Glasgow for the Yorkshire Dales and the job of his dreams, but he'll have to give it everything he's got if he wants to stay. It's his only hope, and then the chaos … a scary downhill drive in Siegfried's car, the squelch across the mud to examine the horse and its hoof … he squats in front of the horse, looks at its leg and it snorts and kicks forward – *whack!* James receives a kick in the chest that sends him flying across the yard and sprawling in dung. At the Aldersons' farm, James is startled by Clive the bull, and while clutching a chicken our hero hops onto the wall – this is the moment he first claps eyes on his future wife. Later, in the Drovers' Arms, he discovers that the local ale is stronger than he's used to, and, back at Skeldale House, he mixes up the cats in their cages. 'It's the wrong cat,' he says to Mrs Hall. 'I don't understand – it said "Jasper" on the cage. I know it did, so how can it be?'

'Maybe because you came home soused,' she says. Mrs Hall has to make good his drunken mistakes, but his future at Skeldale House hangs dangerously by a thread. Mrs Hall does her best to appease Siegfried, as she can see that James could be a good fit if only Siegfried would allow him to flourish … Late that night, local farmer Dick Rudd calls on the practice to help with a difficult calving. James sees it as an opportunity to prove himself and heads out into the night alone, leaving Mrs Hall saying her prayers and watching the clock by the fire at Skeldale. It's James's last shot at redemption. Will he? Won't he? Can he? Yes! Siegfried relents and decides that James can stay after all. The adventure in the dales has only just begun.

❀

'We're not big drinkers.' HANNAH HERRIOT

'No. Neither are we. Special occasions.' SIEGFRIED

❀

'ANOTHER FARNON?'
BY BEN VANSTONE

James treats Mrs Pumphrey's dog, Tricki, and is rewarded with an invitation to her party. And James meets Tristan – whose arrival launches something of a grenade into the already eccentric household, beginning with Tristan crashing Siegfried's Rover. Mrs Hall now has three men to look after.

'ANDANTE'
BY LISA HOLDSWORTH

James and Hugh get stuck driving in opposite directions on a small bridge over a beck. Both cars reverse off the bridge simultaneously … and then go forward at the same time. Meanwhile Tristan is in the marketplace trying to extract bill payments from clients of the practice. He spots Mr Dinsdale … 'Ah, Mister Dinsdale – how fortuitous! Erm, oh my, you have let it build up, one pound and thruppence.' Dinsdale turns sheepish. 'Oh, I don't have any on me now … Well, mother gives me enough for vegetables. Not a penny more, not a penny less.'

'A TRICKI CASE'
BY FREDDY SYBORN AND BEN VANSTONE

Madness ensues when Tricki comes to stay with 'Uncle Herriot' at Skeldale House (James has been concerned about Tricki's flop-bot). The dog looks bloated and glassy eyed and is very overweight. It's clear Mrs Pumphrey has not been following James's advice and has continued to feed him all manner of inappropriate desserts. James tells her it's time for drastic measures and insists on taking Tricki back to Skeldale House for a period of rehabilitation. Mrs Hall is appalled when Tricki arrives in a chauffeur-driven car laden to the gunwales with the dog's favourite luxury cushions; breakfast, lunch and dinner bowls; and favourite toys. James prises the dog from Mrs Pumphrey's loving clutches and orders Mrs Hall to put Tricki on a strict diet and exercise him three times a day. Tricki enjoys running around the yard with Jess and the other animals, and pretty soon the dog starts to shed its puppy fat and has never looked healthier. The same, however, cannot be said for James, Tristan and Siegfried, who start to reap the benefits of the daily hampers of luxury food and alcohol that Mrs Pumphrey is sending for her beloved Tricki.

'He's been so listless, Mr Herriot. I thought he must be suffering from malnutrition, so I've been giving him a little extra between meals. Just to build him up.'

MRS PUMPHREY
REFERRING TO
SPOILT TRICKI

'We don't stop playing because we grow old.
We grow old because we stop playing.'

GEORGE BERNARD SHAW

'ALL'S FAIR'
BY DEBBIE O'MALLEY

Utter chaos in this episode as James discovers that the job of Attending Vet at the Darrowby Show is a poisoned chalice. He's honoured to be asked, taking it as a sign that he has good standing in the community and the dales folk really are starting to accept him. He dons his new crisp, clean veterinary coat and sets out to do the best job possible. But then it's just one problem after another … If it's not the man who is determined to get his dog in the show despite running a dangerously high temperature, it's the woman trying to cheat her 14-hand pony into qualifying for the 13-and-under competition, and when he comes to judge the small-pets category, he finds himself facing a bewildering menagerie of pets. Many of the entrants are young children, their parents staring belligerently over their shoulders. Among them is Helen's younger sister, Jenny, with her pet ferret. There's no way James can please everyone, so he decides on his own method to determine the winner. Instead of judging the pets, James decides to judge the owners. He questions each in turn on the way they treat their pets and awards the top prize to the person who deserves it most. In this case, it's a child with an impeccable knowledge of the correct way to care for his goldfish, and Jenny Alderson is the runner-up. Predictably, it's a choice that doesn't go down well with the assembled crowd. James is confronted by an angry mob in the beer tent as the various people he's upset during the day come back to settle their scores.

'Where on earth did you learn to shoot like that?'
SIEGFRIED

'What did you think we did in the Wrens?
Embroidery?' MRS HALL

Usually the commotion and madness at Skeldale House are observed patiently by Mrs Hall, who is often the one to reinstate order and offer wise, comforting words. 'There's nothing worrying will do for it,' she says. Or 'Don't dwell on what's done when there's things need doing.' As well as 'It'll blow over,' but she can't resist adding in a whisper, 'till the next storm comes rolling in.' Mrs H – as Tristan calls her – accepts that 'some things can't be undone', though she has an instant remedy for most traumas and troubles – 'Better get a brew on.' A cuppa is the cure-all, and soon the steaming teapot is ready for pouring, order restored.

Tea is needed after the encounter between Tristan and Mrs Tompkin (June Watson), whose budgerigar, Peter, needs his beak trimming. Tristan is greeted at the door by Mrs Tompkin, who is elderly and visually impaired but very chirpy. She says, 'Peter's over here, love – poor little fella can barely eat with his beak as it is, and I'm worried about him. He's my only companion, you see. Mind the table.'

Mrs Tompkin moves around furniture, seeing without her eyes. Tristan bumps into it.

Tristan wonders, does Peter's singing keep her company? 'It's a funny thing. Peter has never said owt. I think he's lazy. But I like having him near me.' And then to the budgie: 'I hear your fluttering. Don't I?'

'Don't you worry,' Tristan says. 'We'll soon see him right.' Nothing could be further from the truth. He opens the cage door and clutches Peter – we can tell something is wrong. He opens his hand and … Peter isn't moving.

The deathly silence is punctured by Mrs Tompkin. 'Something the matter, dear?'

He leaves with the dead budgie, telling the partially sighted owner that he'll need his special instruments to trim the beak. Back at Skeldale, Mrs Hall sees him trying to hide the dead budgie from her. 'It's not what it looks like,' he says.

Mrs Hall: Is it a dead budgie?

Tristan: Yes.

Mrs Hall: Then it's exactly what it looks like.

He says, 'I didn't kill it. Well, I suppose I did, but it was an accident. Entirely natural causes. All I did was try to pick it up … It must've been on its last legs and the shock finished him off. I didn't have the heart to tell Mrs Tompkin. This bird's all she has.' His solution: to buy another budgie and hope that blind Mrs Tompkin won't notice the difference. What could be the problem? 'One budgie's not so different from another,' he says.

Mrs Tompkin is thrilled to be reunited with the bird she believes is Peter. But then 'Peter' tweets, which is odd. 'He never used to be able to cheep,' says his owner.

Quick as a flash, Siegfried gives an explanation: 'Peter needed his beak trimmed, and now he has, it's allowed him to find his voice again.'

The chaos of Siegfried's life is reflected by his disorganized accounts, and when Helen moves into Skeldale, she tries to help with them. Helen might not be Darrowby's best cook – actually, she's probably its worst – but she's adept when it comes to getting Siegfried's ridiculously muddled accounts in order. 'Although to the untrained eye it may look a little haphazard,' Siegfried tells Helen as she starts to sort through the mountain of invoices, 'I have to tell you that this system has never let me down yet.'

Siegfried also employs Miss Harbottle (Neve McIntosh) to sort out his messy paperwork (not that he'd admit it's messy) and create a system for the book-keeping. She describes

'You do your own bookkeeping? Invoices? Orders and supplies?'
MISS HARBOTTLE
TO SIEGFRIED

'And I'm sure – with some expert assistance – we could do it all much better.'
SIEGFRIED

herself as an expert at making order out of chaos, and takes on the same challenge. She is horrified to see that Siegfried's cash box is a pewter pot on the mantelpiece, stuffed with crumpled cheques and bank notes. Herriot writes of Miss Harbottle looking 'bereaved' as the challenges mount up, her head often in her hands. She fails to make a real impact and, in the fourth series of this adaptation, has some harsh words for Siegfried: 'You are disorganized, erratic, irresponsible.' His response: 'And you are ignoring the fact that we are vets. We put animals before profits.' (Siegfried is 'complicated', Mrs Hall tells Miss Harbottle, 'but his heart's in the right place'.)

There is mayhem on the roads too, beginning in the first series with James's scary first car journey with Siegfried and continuing with the confusion on the bridge as James and Hugh reverse their cars for each other. Tristan buys a backfiring Morris Cowley from farmer Henry Dinsdale (Mark Noble). 'It's not much to look at,' says Tristan to Siegfried, 'but Dinsdale assures me it's as solid as a tractor.' And Siegfried replies, 'It sounds like one.'

Much of the hilarity in episode five of series four focuses on Richard Carmody's driving lessons, first with James and then with Siegfried. Carmody (played by James Anthony-Rose) is the world's worst driver, but he must learn, because how else can he visit the clients and farmers in the dales? 'The trouble is, James,' says Richard, 'everything about driving makes sense until I actually put it into practice. I'm beginning to come to the conclusion that I was born to be a passenger.'

This is all nonsense as far as Siegfried is concerned. He tells James: 'It's a four-speed Vauxhall, not a bloody seven-man tank! ... Oh, for heaven's sake. I'll teach him myself.' And then we cut to Siegfried in his beloved Rover with Carmody, and you just know it will end badly. Siegfried's advice to the learner: 'It's about confidence. Once you realize that everyone else on the road is an imbecile, it's plain sailing.' (Donald Sinclair had a custom of driving by holding the steering wheel with his elbows, his chin resting in the palms of his hands.) Carmody is motoring cautiously through the lanes,

with Siegfried bellowing orders. 'Look,' says Siegfried, 'forget everything James told you. Just do as I say and you'll be fine. That's it, give it some welly! You'll never cut the mustard if you drive like an old codger! … Show them who's boss. Stay in the middle of the road …' Inevitably, they are heading for a collision with an oncoming Rolls-Royce. The Rover swerves at the last minute and just misses the Rolls-Royce, and the back window is rolled down to show the car's passengers – Mrs Pumphrey and Tricki. Challenges, challenges …

In a sweet twist of irony, it is Mrs Pumphrey who succeeds where Richard Carmody's male colleagues have failed. She is the one who teaches the young vet to drive, thus bringing a sense of order to his chaotic driving.

'Animals, like people,
cannot be simply
tinkered with and fixed
like a wristwatch.'

SIEGFRIED

There are also other sorts of challenges. During Mrs Pumphrey's cricket match, for instance, Samuel West injured himself … twice. He was practising in the nets when he pulled a muscle in his right calf. His leg had to be strapped up and he was limping. Then, and this was on the final day of the shoot, Samuel began a dash from the crease of the pitch and suddenly – ouch! – the Achilles tendon in his left leg snapped. Minutes later, the show's Siegfried was on his way to Accident and Emergency at Ripon Community Hospital. He returned to shoot the final scene from the waist up, as he had a plaster cast on his foot. Jokes were cracked – mostly by Samuel himself – about him being the newest cast member.

There's trouble at Heston Grange, the Aldersons' farm, and it's the sort of trouble that calls for a vet – and quickly! Helen's horse, Candy (played by Aramis), is in foal and is in agony. Candy is also special because she belonged to Helen and Jenny's late mother. (Here we are in episode six of the second series.)

Luckily, James is at the farm visiting Helen (and he's reeking of Mrs Hall's bath salts). He inspects the horse and discovers that Candy's uterus is twisted. 'We're going to need some help.' He sends Jenny to the phone box to call for Siegfried, who arrives with a veterinary pistol, ready to put an end to the suffering. While all of this is going on, Tristan is lying on a sofa with a tumbler of whisky resting on his chest, reading *Biggles Goes to War*. James instructs Siegfried and Mr Alderson to rock Candy from one side to the other, while young Herriot – with his hands in the horse's uterus – holds the foal by its hooves to untwist the uterus and enable the birth. It's an uncommon and life-threatening procedure for horses.

The drama on screen contrasted with the challenges of filming the scenes, and there was an unusual aspect when it came to filming, says Andy Hay, who directed this episode. 'Mark Atkinson, the horse master, said he had a horse that could roll 180 degrees, from one side to the other, legs up in the air. But the horse was Aramis, who is a male.'

Pauline Fowler, the prosthetics expert, was assigned to create a mare's rear end – complete with twitching tail to trick the viewer's eye and add believability. Says Andy: 'We had to do some judicious editing afterwards to remove any male parts. Apologies, Aramis!' They hoped to film the scene in a barn, but this presented two problems: first, horses prefer to give birth outdoors, and they don't like an audience during labour; second, there was too little space in the barn for Aramis to roll on his back from side to side. So they decided to shoot the scene in a field. 'Then I had to find a way of showing that a foal had just been born without having a newborn foal actually on set, or a prosthetic one. A real newborn, of course, was a no-no, and a prosthetic might just look lifeless. But it was in the script, and it was my job to find a way to make it a reality on screen.'

Director Andy Hay and prosthetics expert Pauline Fowler on set.

They located two pregnant mares – one in Yorkshire and another in Devon – that were similar in colour to Aramis. Camera operators were on standby to film these births in a similar setting to Candy's delivery, in a field with trees and dry-stone walls. 'On the day, Aramis was brilliant – he rolled four times for the camera, which meant we managed to get all the shots we needed.' Andy also wanted to shoot a natural reaction from the actors as they witnessed the foal standing minutes after the 'birth'. So he placed his laptop on a chair in the field where they were shooting the scene and played footage of the foal's first steps, which had been captured a week earlier by a camera operator on standby.

The actors playing Helen, Jenny, Mr Alderson, Siegfried, Tristan and James watched the footage of the newborn foal stumbling and standing up for the first time and taking its first suckle. 'As they watched, we filmed their reactions. That meant on screen we had a connection to the birth of Candy's new foal.' Genius! But there was another issue. Aramis had white fetlocks, but the real mother had black fetlocks and a longer mane. It called for more judicious effects in the editing suite. Only one eagle-eyed viewer wrote to point out that he'd spotted the horsey difference.

❦

Langcliffe is a village which sits beside the River Ribble, just a mile north of the bustling market town of Settle. A cotton-spinning mill was built in the village in the 1780s. Langcliffe High Mill was one of Yorkshire's first mills of this kind, and the building remains to this day, along with Watershed Mill, which is now a village visitor centre and a shop that sells outdoor clothing. In series four we meet Sid and Elsie Crabtree (played by Ryan Hawley and Chloe Harris), new to farming because Sid left a job in the mills. 'Mill work did my chest in,' he tells James. 'Can't join up, but I can do my bit here.' And then, referring to his family, he adds, 'And keep this lot safe into the bargain, with any luck.'

The village of Langcliffe (population: about 330) is also home to a disused lime kiln, which was built in the 1870s. Limestone was burned over weeks to produce lime, which was used as mortar in building and by farmers – when added to soil, lime reduces the acidity and improves plant growth. There was a limestone quarry nearby, and about a mile east of the village there's an area of limestone ridges and scars known as Whinskill.

That's where you'll see Samson's Toe. Any of the dales folk at the bar can tell you the myth about the rock – *Ah, Samson was trying to jump across the scar … and broke off his bloody toe.* The 'toe' is about 8 feet high, and geologists would dispute the Samson legend. Instead, they say it is a giant rock made up of greywacke – hard, dark, sharp-angled sandstone comprising quartz, feldspar, clay and fine pebbles. It came from elsewhere and was deposited in this spot when glaciers melted after the last Ice Age and carried rocks from north to south. There are two more boulders nearby and, with Samson's (big) Toe, they

❦

'Stop … hold on! Stop! It's getting tighter. Get her back, quick! We're going the wrong way! Back! On to her chest.'

JAMES

❦

are known as the Whinskill Rocks and also as 'rocking stones'. 'We call 'em the rocking stones because you can rock 'em,' says a gentleman in the pub. 'Or you can – if you're Samson!'

It's only 5 or 6 miles from Malham Lings and its natural formation of cracked limestone 'pavements', a striking feature of the landscape that we see in the first episode when James is left at the crossroads. The 'clints' are the blocks of limestone and the 'grykes' the gaps between them, and together they create a unique sight.

Nearby, in the mossy woods – rich with the scent and sight of wild garlic from late winter to early spring – you can hear Janet's Foss before you see it. Gordale Beck runs into a waterfall and natural pool where, in series one, James goes skinny-dipping … and is more than a little embarrassed when he's caught by Helen. The word 'foss' originates from the Old Norse *fors*, meaning waterfall. As for Janet, well, she is Jennet, queen of the fairies, and she is said to dwell in the cave behind the falls. Many must have gone skinny-dipping in the pool over the centuries, and in the summer it was also the place used by the dales farmers as a natural sheep dip before shearing.

North of Janet's Foss is what was considered one of the natural wonders of the world – Gordale Scar. This gorge and these cliffs, 330 feet high, were formed by torrents of glacial meltwater that cut down through faults in the rock. Successive Ice Ages carved it deeper and deeper. The waterfalls at the heart of the ravine are rich in dissolved limestone, which has run onto the mossy rocks to create the soft tufa screen of Gordale. Gordale Scar is the impressive location for Kate Billings' farm in series three, episode two.

Over the past 1.5 million years, Malham was probably covered at least three times with huge sheets of ice. As these glaciers ground their way over the landscape, they plucked rock from the face of the cove and carried it away, and much later the melting glaciers caused flooding, which, in turn, eroded the landscape. Malham Cove is a 230-feet-high cliff of white limestone a couple of miles from Gordale as the crow flies.

'Morning, James!' HELEN

'Err. Good morning.' JAMES (CAUGHT SKINNY-DIPPING AT JANET'S FOSS)

(Although it's not necessarily a crow in this national park, but it could be a skylark, curlew, lapwing, oystercatcher, red or black grouse, grey partridge, wood warbler, marsh tit, song thrush, ring ouzel … the birds here are happy, varied and vast in number.)

There's a scar above the village, and from there, if you look eastwards across the fields and the river, you can see Giggleswick, so named not because the villagers laughed a lot but after a man called Gickel and his dwelling (wick). The village is renowned for its ancient school of the same name, which was established 500 years ago and is set in 215 acres of countryside. Beyond Giggleswick lies the Forest of Bowland, and beyond that Morecambe Bay and the Irish Sea.

'Has anyone told you how insufferable you are?' JAMES

'Not to my face, no.'
SIEGFRIED

Chat to the local folk in the pubs of the dales and ask about the story of Michael Horner and a terrier dog. The pair played a remarkable role in British archaeology, and it's a tale of hope and determination straight out of the Yorkshire Dales – a story that could well have been told over supper at Skeldale House, and probably by Siegfried.

It was in May 1838 that Horner went rambling with two friends on the cliff range behind Langcliffe. They met John Jennings, who had two terriers with him. They put one of the terriers into what they believed was a fox hole, and it came out of another hole. A week later they returned to the same holes and removed a rock from the entrance to the hole. Michael squeezed himself through the small, narrow entrance. We can only imagine his surprise as he looked around. This was not a hole but a beautiful cave; stalactites hung from the roof of its large chamber; stalagmites covered the walls. No one had set foot in the cave for about 1,100 years, since the time of the Saxon invasion by Edwin of Northumbria in 752. Once it had been a home for a family or clan of Britons who had perhaps blocked it with the boulder and intended to return … but never did.

Joseph Jackson, Michael's boss, was even more keen on exploring the cave and began to excavate, even though he had lacked experience and skill. Over several months, and by candlelight, he gathered valuable artefacts, which included pottery and the bones they had picked. Others visited the cave and helped themselves to relics and stalactites, and soon it was emptied of its beauty and much of its bounty, which lay on the floor of the cave. However, what had been the floor in Saxon times was not the floor in earlier periods. They had, if you like, only scratched the surface. But when Joseph discovered the jawbone of a hyena it became clear that to get to what lay beneath the surface required the skills and talents of archaeologists, who could carefully dig deep into the floor. This was an Aladdin's cave as well as a preserved account of many millennia of climate change in the dales. It was named Victoria Cave after the reigning monarch.

⁂

England, August 1865. Queen Victoria is on the throne. Benjamin Disraeli is serving his second stint as Britain's prime minister. And two months earlier Alexander Graham Bell invented the telephone (though it'll be some time before one is answered with the words 'Hello, Darrowby two-two-nine-seven').

The members of the Settle Caves Committee have gathered to hear the latest developments regarding an archaeological dig that, for the past six years, has been taking place in Victoria Cave. This is one of a few caves just above Settle, a market town in Riversdale in a region known as the West Riding of Yorkshire. The speaker is Richard Hill Tiddeman, a geologist who is thirty-three years old and on his way to becoming one of the leading experts on carboniferous rocks. On this day in Bristol, he has good news. 'Great progress has been made in the past year,' Tiddeman begins, and he explains how, after arduous work digging through huge boulders of limestone and rock, 'bone-beds' have been discovered that contain the remains of humans and of animals that are long extinct. Tiddeman and his team have unearthed the bones of animals that roamed the Earth before the Pleistocene Epoch – the period that ended 11,700 years ago and during which huge ice sheets covered much of the world.

Consider for a moment the animals that James Herriot writes about, among them cows, horses, sheep, dogs and cats – the animals of Britain today. Now consider that one chamber of the cave – Chamber D – 'was choked to the roof with clay and limestone blocks', but after careful excavation 'a magnificent set of bones was found'. This remarkable collection included the specimens (such as bones or teeth) of:

- *Rhinoceros hemitoechus* (a narrow-nosed rhino, which was huge).

- *Elephas antiquus* – a straight-tusked elephant, and tall too (almost 14 feet at shoulder height).

- One piece of the tusk of a hippopotamus.

They also discovered specimens of hyena, bison, fox, red deer, reindeer, pig, goat (or sheep), horse and badger. A collection of bear specimens included two skulls, of which one expert, Professor George Busk, said, 'I think the larger of the two skulls is by far the finest of the kind yet found in this country.' The vertebra of a bear had been hacked with a sharp instrument – evidence of humans. A human fibula was believed to have been found, along with a piece of rib that may also have been human – though both claims were later disputed. But whatever the case, Victoria Cave is one for the must-see list of hopeful tourists, and some of the fascinating and ancient relics discovered there are on display in the Craven Museum in Skipton.

YORKSHIRE SPIRIT
(AND PUDDING)

On a midsummer's afternoon Jim Wight is sitting in a quiet room at the World of James Herriot, the museum dedicated to the life and works of his father, Alf. This visitor centre in Thirsk – at 23 Kirkgate – was once the home and veterinary surgery that inspired Skeldale House, and, just like his father, Jim also worked here. He's having a cuppa with biscuits and reflecting on a vet's life in Yorkshire during his dad's time.

It was a tough life. It still is, I think. I remember Dad's cars. No brakes, no heater. In winters – and they were *proper* winters – don't know how the hell he did it, having to drive up to the Dales. An hour's drive in sub-zero temperatures, and he used to arrive at the farms stupefied with cold. That was his word – *stupefied*. Before he could even function he'd have to go into the kitchen to thaw out. The farmers were all right. They've got layers of coats on and have been mucking out and exercising and milking cows. But the poor old vet has to stand there with syringes, testing for TB. Money? He had nothing. Donald paid him a share of the takings with TB testing, but that's all he got. So he had to do it.

And in fact when he made money as James Herriot – 'cause he were never a greedy man – I said to him: 'You were never interested in money, were you?' And he said, 'I was once. When I didn't have any.'

Other top-selling authors left Britain to avoid paying high rates of tax, and they became tax exiles elsewhere ('just buggered off', as Jim puts it). Alf, however, was always reluctant to leave Yorkshire, so he didn't. Alf was humble and modest and, says Jim, 'He was always a very appreciative man and appreciated every little bit of good fortune that he had. He always regarded himself as lucky. Shortly before he died he told me that he was "an amateur at the writing game"?!'

'Dales farmers are a tough bunch. They know their mind and they're not easily swayed. I should know. I'm one of 'em.'

HELEN

Alf's tone and outlook and his approach to life is reflected in the characters of this adaptation of *All Creatures Great and Small*. We see the Yorkshire spirit in Mrs Hall, even though she was a minor figure in the books. At the outbreak of the Second World War, for instance, she says to Siegfried: 'All wars end eventually. Normal life will return. In the meantime, we must appreciate what we have.' Even if she does wish and pray for that day to come when she is reunited properly with her son, she still values what she has.

During the war the British government launched a campaign that encouraged women to learn how to repair clothes. Materials were in short supply, and clothing factories needed materials to produce uniforms. The Ministry of Information issued a thirty-six-page booklet that contained hints on washing and creating decorative patches to cover holes. It set out its mission:

- To keep clothes looking trim as long as they have to last.

- To renovate children's outgrown clothes so cleverly that none is ever wasted.

- To turn every scrap of good material you possess to advantage.

- To keep your household linen in good repair. To make do with things you already have instead of buying new.

A Second World War era 'Make Do and Mend' booklet prepared by the Board of Trade for the Ministry of Information from 1943.

The booklet, which was produced and written mostly by women, was an impressive collection of tips, advice, know-how and general hints (e.g. never dry coloured materials in strong sunlight, as it bleaches them when they are wet). Today the booklet is a riveting piece of social history. Among its words of wisdom there is, for instance, advice on 'the moth menace', with tips such as: 'Moths like warm, dark cupboards – anywhere, in fact, where they are not disturbed. At least once a month, more often if possible, beat, brush and shake your clothes well, particularly woollens, and air them in the sunlight out of doors. Sun and air kill the grub.'

As for stockings: 'Rinse new stockings through warm water before wearing them, and again after each wearing. You should use your precious soap for washing them only when they are dirty. You can wash them after your bath in the same water, using soap for the soles only. Never iron.' Readers were advised to 'always carry a needle and cotton and mending silk with you – this will save many a ladder in stockings or prevent the loss of buttons; your friends will thank you, too. How many times have you heard someone say, "Has anyone got a needle and cotton?"'

The pamphlet included a rallying call to arms, or to needles: 'Can you help others – for instance, by organizing a group of women with some needlework skill and a little time, to repair the overalls of the local war workers? Ask the welfare or personnel departments of the factories if you can help.' Sewing, knitting and crocheting were promoted. Many women didn't need to be told, because economizing and cutting waste had been instilled in them from childhood. They made the most of what they had.

The campaign's slogan was 'Make Do and Mend', but women such as Mrs Hall and Helen Alderson were already mending and making do. In the run-up to the first series, Ros Little, the costume designer, considered Anna Madeley's character of Mrs Hall and what she would have worn on a housekeeper's salary. 'We tried a variety of colours and came up with some that looked very good on Anna,' says Ros, 'but we all concluded that she had to look like a member of staff rather than a woman of the house. She had to look plain and a little bit intimidating when James first meets her.'

So Anna was given a limited wardrobe and a work look – after all, she is an employee at Skeldale House. Ros adds: 'We also talked about her being *buttoned-up*. Day in, day out, we see her in that cardigan, and it's been mended several times, which is perfect – she'd have darned her own clothes. For a special occasion she breaks into colour and has a beautiful hand-knitted maroon cardigan. She has a range of overalls and floral aprons, which Anna loves.'

'Remember,
I'll only be a few
counties away.' JAMES

'Five. I counted.' HELEN

Anna says that 'it's more about pinny on, pinny off', and she was delighted by Ros's suggestion of the 'lovely old cardigan'. 'We stick to that strong and important sense of homemade,' she adds, 'and Ros has the knowledge and experience to achieve that.'

As the series moves forward in time to the beginning of the Second World War, we see a variety of extras in military uniform. The brilliant website of the Imperial War Museums provides a valuable insight into the sartorial changes at that time. Following the outbreak of war, one of the first noticeable changes in dress was the number of people, both men and women, wearing uniform. 'Around a quarter of the British population was entitled to wear some sort of uniform as part of the armed forces, women's auxiliary forces or one of the numerous uniformed voluntary services and organisations,' says the site.

This increased demand for uniforms put enormous pressure on Britain's textile and clothing industries.

The British government needed to reduce production and consumption of civilian clothes to safeguard raw materials and release workers and factory space for war production. The imposition of clothes rationing was announced by Oliver Lyttleton, President of the Board of Trade, on 1 June 1941. Making the announcement just before a Bank Holiday allowed the Board of Trade time to brief retailers before the shops reopened. The news came as a complete surprise to most people. As with food rationing, which had been in place since 1940, one of the other reasons for introducing civilian clothes rationing was to ensure fairness. Rationing aimed for a more equal distribution of clothing and to improve the availability of garments in the shops.

Each type of clothing item was given a value in points, which varied according to how much material and labour went into

its manufacture. Eleven coupons were needed for a dress, two for a pair of stockings, and eight for a man's shirt or a pair of trousers. Women relinquished five coupons for a pair of shoes, and men had to give up seven coupons for theirs. When buying new clothes, the shopper had to hand over coupons with a 'points' value as well as money. 'Every adult was initially given an allocation of sixty-six points to last one year, but this allocation shrank as the war progressed.

'The coupon allowance was at its lowest during 1945 and 1946. For the eight-month period from 1 September 1945 to 30 April 1946, only twenty-four coupons were issued, effectively allowing the shopper only three coupons a month. Throughout the war, special provisions were made for some people, including manual workers, civilian uniform wearers and diplomats. Had they lived through these times, many members of the *All Creatures* cast – also being theatrical performers – would have also benefited from these special provisions. New mothers were also given fifty coupons. Government publicity offered advice about the complex rationing system. Shoppers were constantly reminded of the need to plan their clothes purchases carefully and make difficult choices between garments of differing coupon values.'

Makeup was not subject to rationing. However, the government applied a luxury tax on it. So apart from having to make do and mend, women also faced a high price for making up their faces.

While Jim was drinking his tea, eating his biscuits and chatting about his dad, visitors to the World of James Herriot were exploring the ground floor, which is just as it was in the old days. Stepping into the kitchen here is like entering Mrs Hall's domain; it is frozen in time.

There was not much freezing in Mrs Hall's kitchen, because while there were ice caves and freezing machines, freezers were yet to become a thing. Meanwhile, fridges were certainly available after the First World War but in very few domestic kitchens. Figures from 1948 show that at that time, only two out of every 100 British households owned such a device. It was known as the 'electric refrigerator', but with Fridgidaire being the best-known manufacturer, the word

'fridge' was adopted but considered a bit common (like 'loo' instead of 'lavatory'). Cookbook authors of the 1970s still opted for 'refrigerator' and avoided the colloquial 'fridge'.

What in heaven's name did people do before they could open the door of a fridge, stand and stare at the shelves and wonder what to eat next? Mrs Hall would know the answer, but *Florence Greenberg's Cookery Book* (published in 1947) also offers valuable advice for the storage of food in the days when it couldn't be chilled.

'Meat', she wrote, 'should be covered with a wire gauze frame; then see that the frame fits the dish tightly, so that flies are unable to enter.' Covers must be kept scrupulously clean. Cheese: 'Wrap the cheese in greaseproof paper, then in damp muslin and hang it in a cool, airy place. Or simply wrap the cheese in muslin wrung out in vinegar. For cooking leave the ends of cheese until really dry, then grate them, place in a screw-topped jar, and keep in a cool larder.'

In hot weather, bottles of milk, Florence advised, should be placed in a basin of cold water – 'cover bottles with muslin, the ends of which should rest in water. Stand in a draught' – while vegetables should be kept in a vegetable rack, with green vegetables wrapped in newspaper. 'Remove the tops of the carrots, turnips, parsnips, and radishes before placing in the vegetable rack. Put onions and shallots in a string bag and hang them where the air can get at them.' Keep lettuce, it was advised, in a saucepan or bowl; cover and stand in a cool dry place or store in plastic bags. Her 'advice regarding the length of time for keeping canned foods': canned milk, fruit and fish in tomato sauce could last one year. Vegetables, honey and jam could last two years. Canned meat and fish in oil could last five years.

Mrs Hall and her fellow cooks of the 1930s didn't have air fryers, microwave ovens, food processors, Microplane graters, handheld blenders or even an electric kettle. They had none of the snazzy gadgets and expensive kitchen luxuries that are available today. Mrs Hall's kitchen inventory would have included these items: whisk, can opener, jelly moulds, mixing

'This is Mrs Hall's domain. Cooks a mean black pudding – makes it herself, you know. Place looks like an abattoir afterwards.'

SIEGFRIED GIVING JAMES A GUIDED TOUR OF SKELDALE HOUSE

bowls, enamel kitchenware such as a bread bin, measuring scales (batteries not included because it was an old-fashioned sort with weights), pastry cutters and pie trimmers. The Aga is the stuff of dreams for many cooks of the twenty-first century, but in the show that magnificent oven is never on (it's just very good at acting like it's on).

A glance inside the cupboards in the frozen-in-time kitchen at 23 Kirkgate shows just the sort of food Mrs Hall and her contemporaries kept as essentials – plenty of tea, naturally; a tin of McDougall's flour; a box of Tate & Lyle granulated sugar ('untouched by hand'); Chivers' Jelly Crystals; a box of Brown & Polson flavoured cornflour to make blancmange; Lion Genuine Ground Mixed Spice; Robinson's Patent Groats, 'gruel of a very superior quality', especially good 'for the weaning of infants and for mothers and invalids', so just the sort of thing Helen would want after the birth of little Jimmy. There was a packet of Colman's mustard powder, to be mixed with water to become a paste and an ideal condiment for Siegfried's English breakfast. Samuel West says, 'I rather like black pudding, but I did one day forget not to have breakfast when we were shooting a breakfast scene. I had to do about seventeen takes of eating black pudding, at the end of which I had turned into one.' (If you are a black pudding devotee and find yourself in Kirkgate, check out Johnson's, the butcher's shop. The Wights tended to buy their meat from Pattison's and Lee's.)

Behind-the-scenes planning for Mrs Hall.

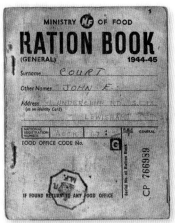

Clothing and food ration books, both issued in 1944 and belonging to a family living in Lewisham.

And perhaps a box of Bournville cocoa, produced by Cadbury's in the Birmingham village of Bournville, or Rowntree's cocoa powder (the same manufacturer had introduced the Aero chocolate bar in 1935, and two years later James Herriot's arrival in Darrowby coincides with the renaming of mini round sugar-coated chocolates called Smarties Chocolate Beans).

A tin of Ovaltine was in just about every British kitchen back then. The malted milk hot drink was invented in Switzerland in 1865 as a tonic for undernourished children but came to prominence in the thirties with the Ovaltineys, a Sunday-evening show on Radio Luxembourg. The catchy theme music began: 'We are the Ovaltineys, little girls and boys …' And they were happy little girls and boys because they all drank Ovaltine. There was an Ovaltineys club, with a nation's children as members. Alf's daughter Rosie was born in 1947 and says, 'One of my earliest memories is of Mum sending me to get sweets from Mr Barnett's shop along Kirkgate, clutching the coupons in my five-year-old hand.'

While Mrs Hall, Helen Alderson and the other women of wartime Britain had to guard the food ration coupons, make do and mend their clothes and forego makeup because it was so expensive, they were also encouraged to give up their cherished aluminium saucepans and pots (although Mrs Hall's array of cooking vessels is mostly copper).

The metal was collected and melted down to make aircraft for the Royal Air Force. Or was it? 'In fact the government did not need any more aluminium,' reports the government's guardian of official documents, the National Archives, 'but it believed the appeal meant people felt that they were doing something to defeat Hitler and helped to keep morale up.' This was the 'Saucepans for Spitfires' campaign, and it was a bit like the environment-friendly recycling campaigns of today's local authorities. Posters urged: 'War job for householders. Wanted at once – old aluminium pots and pans for planes. Ask your local council to collect them.' Leaflets were distributed and posters were plastered on the walls of towns and cities with wording that appealed to the masses, who were eager to do their bit for the war on the Home Front:

- Metal helps to make tanks
- Paper helps to make munitions
- Rubber helps to make tyres
- Bones help to make planes
- Please put out all your paper, metal, bones, rags and rubber for salvage

The food scene in Yorkshire and the dales is so very different today, decades after the end of the Second World War, with rationing a thing of the distant past. This part of the country is energized by the dazzling talent and skills of artisan craftspeople who produce exceptional foods and fabulous drinks. The ever-ravenous Tristan would be agog at what's on offer.

Every July tens of thousands come to eat and drink at the Yorkshire Dales Food and Drink Festival, the biggest of its kind in Britain (every year, that is, except 2020, when the lockdown restrictions of the Covid pandemic put a stop to the event). The inaugural festival took place in Skipton Auction Mart in 2016 and two years later found a permanent home – the meadows and fields of Funkirk Farm, on the outskirts of the town.

Housewives handed over pots and pans to be melted down to make bombers and Spitfires.

'Even with rationing you still make the best breakfast this side of the Pennines.'

JAMES TO MRS HALL AS HE TUCKS INTO A HEARTY COOKED BREAKFAST

'Look, I know this is hard for you both, but your days of mollycoddling me are over. I'm a fully functioning member of society now. You'll just have to find someone else to mother-hen.'

TRISTAN TO SIEGFRIED AND MRS HALL

It has a real carnival atmosphere, with about 250 food and drink producers, a Big Top theatre kitchen for chefs to put on cookery demonstrations, and on another stage tribute bands and DJs give the well-sated crowds a reason to dance. Celebrity chefs and well-known cooks pitch up too; it could be North Yorkshire-born James Martin or Mary Berry or Si King from the Hairy Bikers … This is Yorkshire, where a child would ask, 'What's for tea, Mam?' and the response would be, 'A walk round table and a bite o' each corner.'

There are campers and glampers and caravan dwellers, and all of them arrive hungry and thirsty but none leave that way. En route to the event, you might pass through Harrogate, where there's a hotel, the St George. In the spring of 1978, a sixteen-year-old from a council estate in Leeds began as a kitchen apprentice. Marco Pierre White went on to become the first British chef to win three Michelin stars. The lad did well.

We cannot talk of Yorkshire food without reference to Tristan's favourite, Yorkshire pudding. A batter made of eggs, milk, flour and a pinch of salt is cooked in the oven until nicely inflated, golden and crispy. Traditionally, Yorkshire puddings are served with roast beef, though it's a comforting accompaniment to most roast meats or game. With hot gravy poured into the hole of the pudding, it's fantastic. Her Majesty Queen Elizabeth II was especially keen on a Yorkie with her Sunday lunch after church (she liked the well-done, slightly crispy end slice of the joint).

Yorkshire pudding is so intrinsic to the region's culture that Herriot could not avoid mentioning it, even if his first reference is not complimentary of either the savoury dish or the region from which it takes its name. He writes of how, before coming to Darrowby, he had never been to Yorkshire but had always imagined the county to be 'stodgy and unromantic like its pudding' (though as he makes that initial bus journey towards the Pennines, he is soon captivated by the landscape). He returns to the pudding later on in his memoirs, but this time with stomach-rumbling,

mouth-watering descriptiveness as he writes of a feast at the Bellerbys. James watches the family tuck in, and he becomes increasingly hungry. The meal has begun with each of them devouring a round Yorkshire pudding with a pool of gravy – it is often customary in Yorkshire to serve the pudding like this before the roast, and sometimes it's a meal in itself.

In his 1971 book *The Food of Italy*, American writer Waverley Root credited the origins of this food to the Ancient Romans, who invaded Britain in 43 AD. Three decades later they marched north and conquered the region that we know as York. They named it Eboracum and ruled it for the next three centuries. (Moving ahead 500 years, the Viking warrior Ivor the Boneless conquered the city and it was renamed Jorvik. There are many remnants of the Scandinavian language in this region. Their word *gata*, meaning opening

or road, became *gate* – hence Kirkgate in Thirsk.) Anyhow, Root noted that the Romans did a great deal for their cooking by distributing it widely, and 'the most conspicuous example is that of the first universal basic dish which Etruria gave Rome, pulmentum, which the Legions carried as far as York, England, where it became Yorkshire pudding'. Pulmentum's modern descendant is polenta (now made with cornmeal).

Cooks had been making batter puddings for years, but they were made in a pan without fat. In the sixteenth century, the cooks of Yorkshire began their own revolution by pouring the batter into very hot fat – beef dripping – so that it rose and became crisp on the bottom. The batter was poured into the roasting tin that sat beneath the beef on the spit, therefore catching the drips as it cooked and swelled. While the meat continued to roast, the Yorkshire pudding – or dripping

'Oh good God – not again. Can't you cook anything else?'

SIEGFRIED TO TRISTAN ON BEING SERVED YET ANOTHER MEAL OF MASHED POTATOES

pudding as it would have been known – was eaten, relished with a spoonful of jam or syrup.

William Kitchiner, in *The Cook's Oracle* of 1829, offers a recipe for what he describes as 'Yorkshire Pudding Under Roast Meat, the Gipsies' Way' and sees it as 'an especially excellent accompaniment to a sir-loin of beef, loin of veal – or any fat or juicy joint'. The pudding required a couple of hours' cooking compared with about fifteen minutes in a hot oven today. The 'true Yorkshire pudding', Kitchiner observed, 'is about half an inch thick when done; but it is the fashion in London to make them full twice that thickness'.

There's an extraordinary sight in the market town of Malton, North Yorkshire. A huge mural covers one side of a three-storey house, depicting the recipe for Yorkshire pudding as it appeared in Hannah Glasse's book of 1747, *The Art of Cookery Made Plain and Easy* (subtitled 'Which far exceeds any Thing of the Kind yet published').

Hannah, it is said, was the one who gave the Yorkshire pudding its name. Her recipe is as follows (and, if it's helpful, a quart measures 2 pints, or about 1.1 litres):

> Take a quart of milk, and five eggs, beat them up well together, and mix them with flour till it is of a good pan cake batter, and very smooth; put in a little salt, some grated nutmeg and ginger; butter a dripping or frying pan, and put it under a piece of beef, mutton, or a loin of veal, that is roasting, and then put in your batter, and when the top-side is brown, cut it in square pieces, and turn it, and then let the under-side be brown; then put it in a hot dish as clean of fat as you can, and send it to table hot.

Mrs Hall and other cooks and gourmets of the 1930s would be utterly astonished by the foods that are available in the twenty-first century. They were unaware of many of the foods that we have today, and they enjoyed dishes that have since faded out of fashion – although many of the old classics remain,

thank God. The streets of Leeds city centre are lined with restaurants serving cuisines such as Indian, Japanese, Turkish, Greek … none of which existed in Yorkshire in Herriot's day. Rosie Page recalls, 'When I was very young there was a Chinese restaurant in Harrogate called the Mee Hong. Mum and Dad often went there rather than Betty's for a meal on a Thursday.'

Had the Skeldale House residents fancied fish and chips, they could have driven in the Rover to Yeadon, on the outskirts of Leeds. This town boasted a fish-and-chip shop that opened in 1865. It's gone now, but it could – and did – lay claim to being the longest-running fish-and-chip shop in Britain, though this is contested. A five-minute drive from Yeadon, in Guiseley, Harry Ramsden opened his first fish-and-chip shop in 1928, about a decade before James's arrival in Darrowby. Ramsden would go on to have a chippy empire across the country.

Fish-and-chip shops were exempt from rationing in the Great War and the Second World War, when the period of rationing lasted from 1940 to the early 1950s. Indeed, the meal was regarded as an essential morale booster for the people of Britain, and Winston Churchill described fish and chips as 'our good companions'. (During the D-Day landings, fish and chips were used as a code for soldiers to identify themselves: one would call out 'fish' and – fingers crossed – would receive the response 'chips'.)

Fish and chips are divided by an invisible north–south barrier. In the north, haddock is favoured, and they like 'scraps', the golden pieces of deep-fried batter that collect in the fryer's basket. Cod is a more popular fish in the south, and scraps are not a thing. Northerners like a cup of tea with the meal. Wherever in the country you bought your fish and chips in wartime, north or south, the food was given a liberal splash of vinegar and a generous dusting of salt before being wrapped up in newspaper and handed over the counter. Accompaniments included mushy peas, pickled egg, pickled gherkin or pickled onion. The newspaper wrapping practice kept the food warm but was outlawed in the 1980s, when it became apparent that the ink from the newsprint was toxic. So for chippies around Britain, it really was a case of hold the front page.

For Alf and Joan, fish and chips meant a trip to Bettys, the café and tearoom in Harrogate, which opened shortly after the First World War and has since established itself as the grand dame of Yorkshire's food scene. Invariably they went there when Alf had a half-day on Thursdays and followed the meal with a movie at the cinema. For Alf, Harrogate – with its sheer charm and gentle pace of life – was a relaxing escape from veterinary work.

Jackie Smith talks of Skeldale House having a kind of buttery warmth to it, almost inspired by home baking. 'I used an analogy of a fat rascal, which is a large Yorkshire scone made with currants and cherries, almonds on top. It's utterly delicious and served with butter and jam, and could be eaten on its own. Go past Bettys in Harrogate and you'll see plenty of fat rascals in the window.' A fat rascal sums up Skeldale House – warm, super-saturated colours, much like Ros Little's costumes for the show.

Today's foodies are frequently led by a tick-list of fancy Michelin-starred restaurants, but in Herriot's 1930s Michelin was known mostly as a tyre producer. The hotel and restaurant guide was not introduced to Britain until 1974, the same year Alf saw the publication of his fourth Herriot memoir, *Vet in Harness*. And one of the first British restaurants to be awarded two Michelin stars was the Box Tree, in the lovely spa town of Ilkley, on the southern edge of the dales and surrounded by hills and moorland.

The Sinclair-Wight practice was in Kirkgate, and there's another famous Kirkgate in Yorkshire. The Kirkgate market in Leeds was opened in 1857, and it's just the sort of place you can imagine Mrs Hall shopping during visits to the city. With its fine domed roof, this indoor market is an architectural spectacle, designed by Sir Joseph Paxton, who was also behind the creation of The Crystal Palace in London, built to host the Great Exhibition which was held

'The first time I ever saw you, I was so distracted I got off the bus in the middle of nowhere … I never imagined for a second this is where we'd end up.'

JAMES TO HELEN
THE NIGHT BEFORE
THEIR WEDDING

in 1851. One day in 1884 a chap called Michael Marks, who lived in Leeds, opened a penny bazaar in this market. 'Don't ask the price. It's a penny!' That was his slogan, and he sold haberdashery essentials, cutlery, confectionery, basic food items such as spices and flour, and cheap toys. A decade later Michael went into partnership with Tom Spencer, and there you have it – the birth of the world-renowned high street retailer Marks & Spencer.

But busy little Market Place in Darrowby is Mrs Hall's preferred shopping zone, and it's on her doorstep. How very different the shopping basket would have been back then. As a nation, we were decades away from truly discovering the delights of, say, olive oil, and if you like avocado toast, consider that this fruit would never have been seen on a market stall (or anywhere in Britain for that matter) at that time, as it wasn't until the 1960s that it really became available here. Instead Mrs Hall's basket would have been laden with seasonal produce, so a winter shop might include potatoes, parsnips, Brussels sprouts, carrots, apples and pears, as well as ingredients such as flour and sugar for her much-adored scones and shortbread.

Mrs Hall and Helen – and Dash and Jess – are alone together in the kitchen at Skeldale. (It is series four, episode four, written by Maxine Alderton.) Earlier in the episode we've seen Mrs Hall carting a heavy basket of wet laundry towards the back door. Pregnant Helen is at the table, flicking through Mrs Hall's book of recipes, while Mrs Hall is removing a batch of scones from the Aga. 'I always tend to wing it,' says Helen, referring to her notorious style of cooking.

'Follow each step,' advises wise Mrs Hall. 'You can't go wrong.' Helen turns the page to the recipe for shortbread, and it's marked by a child's floury handprint. 'If you can read it for Edward's mucky paws, of course.'

It was an era in which women kept their own cherished books of recipes and passed them down to daughters, granddaughters. The pages consisted of handwritten recipes from family and friends, and others that were cut from newspapers and magazines and then stuck into the book with glue – the original cut and paste. It was a scrapbook for the cook. Mrs Hall's bookshelves are not lined with cookbooks like you may see in today's kitchens, because most women owned perhaps two or three cookery books. The housewife who bought a new oven tended to receive a well-produced cookery book as a small gift from the oven manufacturer.

Then there was Isabella Beeton's cookery book, an enduring classic from Victorian times. Originally published as *Beeton's Book of Household Management*, it became a popular wedding gift for the bride and was just the sort of thing Mrs Hall would have received when she married Robert before the Great War. Over the years Mrs Beeton's recipes were tweaked and tampered with and eventually the book became a rather sad and pale imitation of the original, but still it sold to quite a few generations. Mrs Hall is very much of the Beeton

approach to cooking. 'A place for everything, and everything in its place,' was Mrs Beeton's mantra. She believed that 'one of the chief considerations of life is, or ought to be, the food we eat, for our physical well-being depends mainly on diet'. They are words with which Mrs Hall would thoroughly agree (though maybe she'd include our mental wellbeing too).

Good Cookery by W. G. R. Francillon is also the sort of book that Mrs Hall and her contemporaries might have owned. Flicking through the pages, we can see dishes that might have been cooked and served at Skeldale and many other homes in 1930s Britain. It features soups of chestnut, mutton, ox-tail and calf's head. Rabbit was often on the menu, and *Good Cookery* includes recipes for rabbit that's boiled, jugged, stewed, baked, roasted or turned into a ragout.

There are plenty of recipes for jellies, meringues and sweet puddings such as syrup sponge and bread-and-butter pudding, although the sticky toffee pudding, now world-renowned, had yet to make a name for itself. Scones are given an amount of space of which Mrs Hall would approve, with recipes for Balmoral scones (cut into triangles), butter scones with currants, cream scones, drop scones (or 'Scotch pancakes'), potato scones, sultana scones, tea scones, treacle scones and wholemeal scones … A chapter of vegetarian recipes includes dahl, risotto, succotash (made with haricot beans and sweetcorn) and macaroni cheese (which has stood the test of time and is often referred to as 'mac and cheese').

Cookery books of Mrs Hall's era often included blank pages at the back to be used for cutting and pasting recipes from newspapers. Wartime newspapers ran inspirational recipes for the cooks at home. These were short and contained few ingredients because … well, there weren't many ingredients around. They included recipes for digestive biscuits, 'rice cheese', lentil soup, 'savoury steak', date gingerbread that required no sugar, Christmas pudding, Christmas cake, and one for cheese flan, which was introduced like this: 'Before the cheese ration is reduced again, try this flan as a savoury for lunch or as a supper dish.'

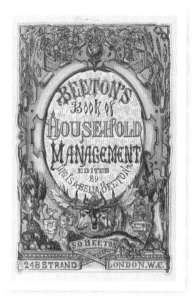

Iconic: the pioneering compilation of recipes and household advice by Isabella Beeton, first published in 1861.

'It's Highland shortbread.
I thought it would remind
you of home.' HELEN

'You didn't bake them,
did you?' JAMES

The economizing and rationing of the Second World War gave us crumble: stewed fruits (usually chopped apples) poured into a dish and covered with a mixture of flour, sugar and margarine before being baked in the oven until the topping is golden and crunchy. The margarine has since been replaced by butter, and cooks sometimes replace flour with oats, but crumble remains a traditional national dish.

'Mustn't keep Mrs Hall waiting,' says Siegfried to James outside the Drovers'. He's referring to another feast which has been lovingly made by the housekeeper, and the men need to down their pints so they can dash to the table at Skeldale. 'I think she wants to make sure you never dream of going away again.'

Actually, the food we see on the show is cooked mostly by food stylist and home economist Bethany Heald, who has also worked on *Happy Valley* and *Gentleman Jack* and as home economist on *MasterChef* and *Great British Menu*. Bethany shares her culinary wisdom and know-how with Anna Madeley. We salivate as we watch the second series, with Mrs Hall piping cream onto Tristan's favourite blancmange. It was Bethany who taught Anna how to pipe like a proficient pastry chef. Plus, there are those happy, heaving, hearty English breakfasts, as well as trays of freshly baked cakes, scones and shortbread. Compliments must go to the cook, Bethany! Anna says: 'I never complain about eating breakfast for one take after another, though you do have to think ahead and be careful not to get too full.'

Bethany says: 'Often when they're eating, there's take after take after take, and all the different angles to film.' In a typical breakfast scene the actors might go through the equivalent of about forty normal-sized breakfasts as they appear to eat. 'Sometimes the actors get really miffed because there's too much dialogue, so they're not allowed to eat because they can't rechew and say their lines. There was one scene when the table had to be laden with breakfast and they weren't allowed to eat anything.' The minute the scene ended 'all of them dived in and demolished these breakfasts that they'd been drooling over for the last two hours'.

'My mother used to
despair at my mucking
about with animals.
Still does.'

JAMES

Off set, cast and crew are fed by Yorkshire-based location caterers Daru TV and Film, which is run by Danny Janes and Russ Kellet. The ensemble cast's WhatsApp group messages often focus on the Daru's daily offerings, which include afternoon tea. The chocolate brownies are especially popular. Nick Ralph and Rachel Shenton can't resist these particular treats, but to keep the calories down and alleviate the guilt they share one brownie between the two of them.

Mrs Hall leans against the train window, watching dusk fall over the hills and lakes as she moves ever closer to Darrowby. She is returning home, having just seen Edward for that brief encounter at Keighley railway station when he has been given a short spell of leave. She tells her son: 'You need to know how much you mean to me – from the moment you were born to this moment right now – that's never ceased one bit … I never stopped loving you.'

For their reunion – in episode five of series three – she took along a tin of shortbread, Edward's favourite. After their emotional encounter, he boards a train back to his barracks. As Mrs Hall hands her son the tin of shortbread … he drops it. He calls out to her from the window, but a loud blast of the train's horn makes his parting words inaudible. She yells out, 'What did you say? … Edward? Say that again. I can't hear you. What is it? … Edward?' The train disappears into the distance, leaving Mrs Hall on the platform, sobbing as she bends down to pick up the tin and the scattered pieces of shortbread. It is Penny, a deaf lady, who answers her question. Penny has lip-read Edward's words. 'He said, "I love you, Ma."' Mrs Hall's eyes fill with tears, and they trickle down her cheeks. She wipes them away. Penny plants her arm around Mrs Hall. Mrs Hall lets herself be comforted.

That evening, once she is back home, Tristan (in an apron) has a surprise shepherd's pie in the oven, and as she sits down with Siegfried, Tristan brings them a cup of tea, a biscuit on the saucer. 'Ah,' says Siegfried, delighted. 'Mrs Hall's shortbread. Thank you.' And he tells her: 'I don't think any of us know quite how to express our gratitude to you, Mrs Hall. Believe me.'

Mrs Hall laughs softly and then lets out a sigh of happiness. Happy, after all this time, to have been reunited with her son. Happy to be back at Skeldale House. It's a make-do-and-mend life for now, but, as she says, all wars must end. And then they will all be back together, here in the Yorkshire Dales: James and Helen with baby Jimmy; Tristan and his mischievous smile; Siegfried, brusque but loyal and well meaning, trailed by a cloud of pipe smoke; and Mrs Hall with her four-legged companion, Jess.

They will be together in Darrowby, united to take on the trials of the veterinary practice, the challenges of parenthood, and the difficult animals. Or rather, the animals are the easy part. It's the people who cause all the bother.

James, newly enlisted into the Royal Air Force, is waiting at the bus stop. This time the red-and-white charabanc will be taking him away from Darrowby. He is on his way to the air

force base at Brize Norton. 'Won't be the same without you,' says Mrs Hall. They hug, and she whispers to him: 'Don't let it change you.'

'I won't.'

James boards the bus to Keighley, the same bus on which he met Helen when he first came to Darrowby. And, as it pulls away, James reaches into his coat pocket and pulls out a photograph. It shows Helen and James on their wedding day.

War will separate them. Conflict will bring hardship, suffering and ill-fortune into their lives. These are the certainties of this looming uncertainty. But their love for each other will keep them going. James studies the picture, and we listen as he recites Robbie Burns's romantic ballad, 'My Love Is Like a Red, Red Rose'. It is the centuries' old anthem of hope; a young man's promise that, whatever adversity he faces, one day he shall come back, to be reunited sweetly with his bonnie lass, his only love.

O my love is like a red, red rose
That's newly sprung in June;
O my Love is like the melody
That's sweetly played in tune.

As fair art thou, my bonnie lass,
So deep in love am I;
And I will love thee still, my dear,
Till a' the seas gang dry.

Till a' the seas gang dry, my dear,
And the rocks melt wi' the sun;
And I will love thee still, my dear,
While the sands o' life shall run.

And fare thee well, my only love!
And fare thee well a while!
And I will come again, my love,
Though it were ten thousand mile.

James does come back, and far sooner than either he or Helen had expected. It is thanks to his veterinary skills that he is reunited with his wife.

James has treated the broken flight feather of Georgie, the falcon and mascot at the RAF base. 'I've never treated a bird like this before,' says James to Flight Officer Woodham. 'Usually it's chickens, maybe the odd parakeet. This is

something completely different.' By Boxing Day Georgie is well on his way to recovery and Woodham, in a moment of good spiritedness, drives James to Darrowby. Our hero has two days' leave.

'Helen! Helen!' An over-excited James brushes past Siegfried and Mrs Hall, and dashes up the stairs of Skeldale House. There's no time for them to tell him the good news. He bursts into the room, kisses and hugs his wife who is in her dressing gown on the bed. 'Oh God,' says James, 'I've missed you – I've missed you so much. I needed to see you. I tried to get to you…'

'Be careful with me,' says Helen. 'Let go now, James.'

'What's wrong? What're you still doing in bed?' And then he realises… Their baby has been born. Helen picks up the baby from the cot and carefully hands him to James. It's a moment of tenderness between new father and child. 'I'd like you to meet your son,' says Helen. James is transfixed. 'You gave me a little boy.'

Helen beams as James kisses baby Jim on the forehead, and then he says: 'Funny looking thing, isn't he?'

'I suppose every foal that's born is a beauty,' replies Helen.

James: 'Near enough.'

It is a little later that same day and the Christmas episode of the fourth series is drawing to a festive close. Snowflakes are falling over Darrowby. James and Helen are standing on the steps of Skeldale House. He puts an arm around Helen and she holds him close, their foreheads resting against each other. Their little baby is between them, in James's arms.

'You all right?' asks James, and Helen replies, 'I am now.'

'I love you so much,' he says.

'I love you, too.'

Helen runs her fingers over little Jim's forehead. 'Let's get you in before you get cold …'

PICTURE CREDITS

KEY LOCATIONS

Skeldale House (interior)
    A studio set near Harrogate
Skeldale House (exterior)
    Arncliffe Village
Darrowby, village
    Grassington
The Drovers' Arms (exterior)
    Devonshire Arms, Grassington
The Drovers' Arms (interior)
    The Green Dragon Inn, Hardraw
Herriot household, Glasgow
    Bradford Industrial Museum, Bradford
Waterfall (James swimming)
    Janet's Foss, Malham Lings
Mrs Pumphrey's mansion
    Broughton Hall, Skipton
Railway stations
    Keighley (Glasgow Station) and Oakworth
    (Darrowby Station)
G. F. Endleby, grocer
    The Stripey Badger Bookshop, Grassington
Glasgow Streets
    Cater Street, Bradford
Benson's Farm, yard and fields
    Kettlewell
Darrowby Village Hall (Daffodil Ball)
    St Wilfrid's Church Hall, Harrogate
Sebright Saunders Estate / Sennor Fell
    Sawley Hall Estate, Ripon
The Renniston
    Ripley Castle, Ripley

Ritz Cinema (exterior)
    Westgate, Thirsk
Canal towpath (exterior) and Mrs Donovan's canal
    boat
    Newton Grange, Skipton
Pumphrey cricket pitch, rear lawn and marquee
    Studley Royal Cricket Club (second pitch)
    Fountains Abbey Deer Park, Harrogate
Hulton Hall and Stables
    Norton Conyers, Ripon
Alderson's Farm (exterior)
    Yockenthwaite Farm, Hubbersholme
Ministry of Agriculture
    Crescent Gardens, Harrogate
Pandhi's House
    Bradford Industrial Museum, Bradford
RAF Training School
    Yorkshire Air Museum, Elvington

Overleaf: The cast and crew for series five.